World's Great Personalities

Published by
Lotus Press Publishers & Distributors

World's Great Personalities

Shalini Mathur

Lotus PRESS
4735/22, Prakash Deep Building,
Ansari Road, Daryaganj,
New Delhi - 110002

Lotus Press Publishers & Distributors
Unit No. 220, 2nd Floor, 4735/22, Prakash Deep Building,
Ansari Road, Darya Ganj, New Delhi- 110002
Ph : 41325510, 98118-38000
• E-mail : lotuspress1984@gmail.com
www.lotuspress.co.in

World's Great Personalities

ISBN: 978-81-8382-220-6

Printed & Published by : **Lotus Press Publishers & Distributors,** New Delhi-02

Preface

This riveting book chronicles the lives of people who have influenced the course of history over the last 2000 years: statesmen, scientists, inventors, artistes, sports heroes, leaders, political thinkers, inventors, painters, entertainers, movie celebrities, writers, musicians and composers, political leaders, philosopher, religious leaders, mathematicians and many more.

Some of these include Mother Teresa, Guru Nanak, Akbar the Great, Salim Ali, Aryabhatta, Beethoven, Kiran Bedi, Bradman, Baille, Chaplin, Columbus, Descartes, Dickens, Walt Disney, Edison, Gandhi, Bill Gates, Hitchcock, Edmund Hillary, R.K. Laxman, Florence Nightingale, A.R. Rahman, Ramakrishna, G.B. Shaw, Tagore.

Provides authentic information about famous personalities or inspirational people's life in a concise yet comprehensive manner.

This book is vital reading for everyone who wants a fuller and broader understanding of the great personalities who have shaped out world.

Author

Content

1

Akbar the Great

(1543-1605)

Emperor Akbar, also known as Akbar the Great or Jalaluddin Muhammad Akbar, was the third emperor of the Mughal Empire. He made significant contributions in the field of art. Apart from commencing a large collection of literature, he also commissioned a number of splendid buildings during his reign. He practised tolerance aimed at Hindu-Muslim unification through the introduction of a new religion known as Din-i-Ilahi.

Akbar was born in Umarkot (Pakistan) on 15 October 1542.

He spent his youth learning to hunt, run and fight, and never found time to read or write. He was the only great Mughal ruler who was illiterate. Despite this, he had a great desire for knowledge and hence his interest in art, architecture, music and literature. He had his books read out to him by his courtiers. Therefore, even though unable to read, he was as knowledgeable as the most learned of scholars

Akbar was only thirteen when his father died of an unfortunate accident in the palace at Delhi. So on 14 February 1556, he succeeded the throne, in the midst of a war waged by Sikandar Shah for the Mughal throne.

For the next five years Bairam Khan (regent) helped Akbar rule the kingdom. In 1561 Bairam Khan died and Akbar took over the government in his own hands.

He won the allegiance of the Rajputs and Hindus by appointing them to important military and civil positions, conferring honours upon them, and marrying a Hindu princess, Jodhabai.

During his reign, Akbar managed to subdue almost all of India. His kingdom extended from Afghanistan to the Bay of Bengal and from the Himalayas to the Godavari River.

The first battle fought by Akbar was against Sikandar Shah Suri of Punjab. However, when Akbar was busy leading an assault against him, Hemu, a Hindu warrior, launched an attack on Delhi, and claimed the capital. On the advice of his general, Bairam, Akbar launched an attack on Delhi and reclaimed the city. On 5 November 1556, Akbar fought the Second Battle of Panipat against General Hemu. Following soon after was the battle with Sikandar Shah at Mankot. In 1557, Adil Shah, who was the brother of Sikandar, died in a battle in Bengal.

In 1579 Akbar abolished the *jizya,* a tax imposed on all but the poorest non-Muslims. His greatest achievement was the establishment of a very effective administrative system. He was also very tolerant towards other faiths and religions and let people practise their faiths independently. He also was a reformist and abolished laws that were unfair.

Akbar was a great patron of literary works and scholars. Under his rule art and architecture flourished. Miniature paintings from his era are considered to be masterpieces. His court had numerous scholars of the day who are well known as *Navaratnas* (Nine Jewels). He patronised such scholars as Birbal, Abul Fazl and Tansen. He had a library of over 24,000 books and he set up a department for translation in his court. He ordered the translation of the *Ramayana* and the *Mahabharata.*

He practised tolerance aimed at Hindu-Muslim unification through the introduction of a new religion known as *Din-i-Ilahi* in 1582. It contained the teachings mainly from Hinduism, Islam and Christianity.

As his reign progressed Akbar moved ever further from Islamic orthodoxy. Later he took to inviting clerics from various religions, including Portuguese Jesuits from Goa, to debate their faiths. He built the Red fort at Agra and also Fatehpur Sekri in honour of Sheikh Salim Chishti.

Akbar fell ill and died of slow poisoning on October 27, 1605. His body was entombed in a magnificent mausoleum at Sikandra city, near Agra.

❖❖❖

2
Mohammad Ali

(1942-)

Mohammad Ali is a retired American boxer and former three-time World Heavyweight Champion. As an amateur, Ali won a gold medal at the Olympic in the light heavyweight division gold medal. As a professional, he became the only man to have won the linear heavyweight championship three times. In 1999, Ali was crowned "Sportsman of the Century" by Sports Illustrated and the BBC.

Mohammad Ali (Cassius Marcellus Clay) was born on 17 January 1942 in Louisville, Kentucky.

He started boxing in junior high at the age of 12. A black trainer named Fred Stoner taught him the science of boxing and to move with the grace of a dancer. By the time Ali reached high school, he already intended to be a prizefighter and hoped to box in the Olympics. As an amateur boxer, Ali attracted notice in 1960 by winning the Amateur Athletic Union light heavyweight and Golden Gloves heavyweight championships.

At the Rome Olympics in 1960, Ali crushed his opponents to win a gold medal in the light heavyweight division, and later tossed it into a river because he was disgusted by racism in America. Ali decided to change his religion and joined the Nation of Islam (Black Muslims), taking the Muslim name Muhammad Ali in 1963.

After turning pro, Ali defeated his first opponents. Then on 25 February 1964, he fought, Sonny Liston in a match of classic contenders for the heavyweight championship of the world. The Miami fight almost single-handedly restored intelligence and balance to boxing. Chanting the war cry "Float like a butterfly, sting like a bee" for weeks, he won the fight in seven rounds to become heavyweight champion of the world.

Ali defended his title nine times from 1965 to 1967 and became the world heavyweight champion after outpointing World Boxing Association (WBA) champion Ernie Terrell on 6 February 1967.

In 1967, he was inducted into the military, but he refused to serve, saying his religious beliefs forbade him to fight. After a long court battle, Ali was convicted of draft evasion and sentenced to five years in jail and fined $10,000 fine, but in another lawsuit in 1970, a judge ruled that Ali could still box professionally.

In November of 1970 Ali fought Jerry Quarry in Atlanta and was victorious. He spent the next four years fighting other champions, winning all but one fight to Ken Norton. He also won a unanimous decision over Frazier on 28 January 1974, but Frazier had lost the heavyweight title to George Foreman. So Ali next had to fight Foreman.

Millions of people gathered at the stadium in Kinshasa in Zaire on 30 October 1974 to watch the fight between Ali and Foreman, staged as "The Rumble in the Jungle". In round eight, Ali knocked out Foreman. He had regained the undisputed world heavyweight title.

Taking time to reflect on the tumult of his fifteen-year boxing career, Ali co-wrote his autobiography, *The Greatest: My Own Story*, in 1975.

After defending his heavyweight title six times—including a third fight with Joe Frazier—Ali lost it to Leon Spinks on 15 February 1978 in a split decision. He regained the WBA title from Spinks seven months later in a unanimous decision, becoming the first boxer to win the heavyweight championship three times.

In 1979 Ali announced his retirement, at that point having lost only three times in 59 fights, but he returned to fight World Boxing Council champion Larry Holmes in 1980 and Trevor Berbick of Canada in 1981, losing both. Ali then retired permanently.

In 1984 he was suffering from Parkinson's disease. He was selected to light the Olympic flame at the 1996 summer games in Atlanta, Georgia. He approached the unlit saucer with his flaming torch, his free arm trembling visibly from the effects of Parkinson's.

Toward the end of his boxing career, and afterward, his ambitions took a decided turn toward statesmanship. In 1980 he cast his lot with the Democratic Party, supporting then-Presidential candidate Jimmy Carter.

He has contributed to countless, diverse charities and causes. Although Parkinson's syndrome has slowed him down, he still remains active — raising money for the Muhammad Ali Foundation and frequently appearing at sports tributes and fund-raisers.

❖❖❖

3

Salim Ali

(1896-1987)

Salim Ali, nicknamed 'The Birdman of India', and also known as the 'Grand Old Man of Indian Ornitholog'', is the recipient of the J. Paul Getty Wild Life Conservation Prize for his contributions to ornithology. He was won several national honours and awards as well.

Salim Moizuddin Abdul Ali, better known as Salim Ali, was born on November 12, 1896. Orphaned at a very young age, he was brought up by his maternal uncle. He spent his childhood in a large house. As a child he was given an expensive Daisy air gun as a present, and he spent all his time shooting sparrows around the house. One day he noticed that one of the sparrows he had shot had a yellow throat. At the Bombay Natural History Society (BNHS), the honorary secretary, W.S. Milliard told him that the bird was the Yellow Throated Sparrow. Milliard also told him about the variety of sparrows. The conversation left a deep impact on the young boy. That day he decided that he wanted to know everything there was to learn about birds. He was going to be an ornithologist.

As a young man Salim had to face years of unemployment and hardship. There were hardly any jobs available for ornithologists in India and so in 1919 he moved to Burma to look after the family mining and timber business. It was a rewarding experience for the naturalist as there were endless opportunities for exploring the forests of Burma.

He went to Germany and trained under Professor Stresemann, an acknowledged ornithologist in Berlin, for some advanced training in stuffing and skinning of birds.

He returned to India and set up a small house at Kihim, across the harbour. It was a quiet place set in the midst of trees. When the monsoon came that year, Salim found a colony of weaver birds on a tree near his house. Not much was known about weaver birds then and it was a golden opportunity for him to study them. For three or four months he patiently watched the activities in the colony for hours on end.

The publication of his findings in 1930 brought him recognition in the field of ornithology and he won high acclaim. *The Book of Indian Birds* that he wrote contained lively descriptions and colour pictures of every species. It made spotting a bird easy for the layman.

In 1948 he began an ambitious project in collaboration with S. Dillon Ripley, an ornithologist of international repute, to bring out in ten volumes *Handbook of the Birds of India and Pakistan.* The work contains all that is known of birds of the subcontinent, their appearance, where they are generally found, their breeding habits, migration and what remains to be studied about them.

❖❖❖

4

Vishwanathan Anand

(1969-)

Viswanathan Anand is an Indian chess grandmaster and the current World Chess Champion. He is one of four players in history to break the 2800 mark on the FIDE rating list. In 2007 he was awarded the Padma Vibhushan. He is also the first recipient of the Rajiv Gandhi Khel Ratna Award (1991-92), India's highest sporting honour.

Viswanathan Anand was born on December 11, 1969 in Chennai, India.

Anand completed his schooling from Don Bosco School, Chennai and B.Com from Loyola College, Chennai. He was conferred the Honorary Doctorate degree by the Jawaharlal Technology University at the age of 18.

Anand started playing chess at the age of six. His first national level success came at the age of 14 when he won the National Sub-Junior Chess Championship in 1983. He was the champion of the National Junior Championship (under 19) from 1983 to 1986. He was the winner of the Asian Junior Championships for two consecutive years - 1984 and 1985.

Anand became the first Asian to win the 1987 World Junior Championship and earned the grandmaster title in 1988 at the age of 18. (In India however this record has been beaten by another chess prodigy P.Harikrishan.) He made it to the quarter finals of the FIDE Candidates Tournament in 1991.

Anand won the Reggio Emilia Tournament in 1991. He lost to Kasparov in the Professional Chess Association World Chess Championship final in 1995. He has won three consecutive Advanced Chess tournaments in Leon since 1998.

Anand became the first Indian to win the 2000 FIDE World Chess Championship title. He lost the title when Ruslan Ponomariov won the FIDE knockout tournament in 2002. He tied for second with Peter Svidler in the FIDE World Chess Championship 2005. He was also the winner of the 2003 FIDE World Rapid Chess Championship.

Anand is the only player to win the Corus Chess Tournament titles five times. He was the winner of the Monaco Amber Blindfold and Rapid Chess Championships in the years 1994, 1997, 2003, 2005 and 2006. He has also won the Linares Tournament twice (1998, 2007) and the Dortmund Tournament thrice (1996, 2000 and 2004).

Anand's memorable achievements in the year 2007 were wining the Linares-Morelia Tournament and the World Chess Championship.

He was at the top of the world rankings five out of six times, from April 2007 to July 2008. In October 2008, he dropped out of the world top three ranking for the first time since July 1996.

Anand has signed an endorsement deal with Parle Products Private Limited. He is the global ambassador of Spastics Society of India (Earlier known as Vidyasagar) and National Institute of Information Technology Ltd (NIIT).

Anand has won several awards and honours: Arjuna Award (1985), Padma Shri Award (1987), National Citizens Award (1987), Soviet Land Nehru Award (1987), Shri Rajiv Gandhi Award – Outstanding Sports Person (1988), Rajiv Gandhi Khel Ratna Award (1991-1992), K. K. Birla Award – 1995 Person of the Year, Sportstar Millenium Award (1998), Padma Bhushan Award (2000), James de Oro – an honour given by the Lanzarote Government in Spain in 2001, Chess Oscar four times (1997, 1998, 2003 and 2004), and Padma Vibhushan (1907).

He has also won the 1998 Book of the Year Award for his book *My Best Games of Chess* given by the British Chess Federation.

He was one of the nominees of NDTV 'Indian of The Year 2007' and CNN-IBN 'Indian of The Year 2007' in the Sports Category. He was declared the 'Sportsperson of The Year 2007' in January 2008.

❖❖❖

5

Hans Christian Andersen

(1805-1875)

Hans Christian Andersen was a Danish writer and poet. He wrote many poems, plays, stories and travel essays, but is best known for his fairy tales of which there are over one hundred and fifty, published in numerous collections during his life and many still in print today.

Andersen was born on 2 April, 1805 in Odense, on the Danish island of Funen, Denmark. His early life was full of great sadness. His family was very poor.

After the death of his father, Andersen travelled to Copenhagen to pursue an acting career at the Royal Theatre. Under the patronage of the Theatre's Jonas Collins, he attended the Copenhagen University which were formative but difficult years for him.

Andersen turned his pen to writing poems, plays and stories, his first poem "The Dying Child" published in the *Copenhagen Post* in 1827.

The Improvisatore (1835) received international acclaim for Andersen, published by the University, and with this encouragement he set off on his literary career.

Many of Andersen's plays including *Love at St. Nicholas' Tower* and *The Mulatto* were performed at the Royal Theatre. He travelled extensively throughout Europe during his life and wrote a number of travel books including; *A Walking Tour from the Holmen Canal to the Eastern Point of the Amager* (1829); *Shadow Pictures* (1831), *O.T.: Life in Denmark* (1836), and *Pictures of Sweden* (1851).

He received the Knighthood of the Red Eagle from King Friedrich Wilhelm IV of Prussia in 1846, and the Maximilian Order of Art and Science from King Maximilian II of Bavaria in 1859. He was made an Honorary Citizen of Odense in 1867.

Andersen's fame rests on his *Fairy Tales and Stories*, written between 1835 and 1872. *Tales, Told for Children*, appeared in a small, cheap booklet in 1835. The third volume, published in 1837, contained 'The Little Mermaid' and 'The Emperor's New Clothes'.

Among Andersen's other best known tales are 'Little Ugly Duckling', 'The Tinderbox', 'Little Claus and Big Claus', 'The Princess and the Pea', 'The Snow Queen', 'The Nightingale', and 'The Steadfast Tin Soldier'. With these collections, inspired by the great tradition of the *Arabian Nights* on the other hand, and *Household Tales*, collected by the brothers Grimm, Andersen became known as the father of the modern fairytale.

Other Andersen titles include *Only a Fiddler* (1837), *A Poet's Bazaar* (1842), *A Christmas Greeting to My English Friends* (1847), *The Two Baronesses* (1848), *To Be or Not To Be* (1857), and *New Tales and Stories* (1858-59).

Andersen's tales were translated throughout Europe, with four editions appearing in the UK in 1846 alone. He wrote as many as 350 stories. His identification with the unfortunate and outcast made his tales very compelling.

Andersen died on 4 August, 1875 in Copenhagen, Denmark.

❖❖❖

6

Aristotle

(384-322 BCE)

Aristotle was a Greek philosopher, a student of Plato and teacher of Alexander the Great. He wrote on many subjects, including physics, metaphysics, poetry, theatre, music, logic, rhetoric, politics, government, ethics, biology and zoology.

Aristotle was born at Stagira, Thrace in 384 B.C.

At the age of 17, he went to Athens and joined Plato's school, where he stayed until Plato's death in 347. A few years later, he became the tutor to the young prince of Macedon, Alexander the Great.

Aristotle returned to Athens three years later, founded his own school, the Lyceum, and taught and studied there for twelve years.

Although he studied under Plato, Aristotle fundamentally disagreed with his teacher on just about everything. Aristotle believed that the world could be understood at a fundamental level through the detailed observation and cataloging of phenomenon. As a result of this belief, he literally wrote about everything: poetics, rhetoric, ethics, politics, meteorology, embryology, physics, mathematics, metaphysics, anatomy, physiology, logic, dreams, and so forth.

In addition to studying everything, Aristotle was the first person to really think out the problem of evidence. In his treatise on animals, he studied over five hundred species; in studying government, he collected and read 158 individual constitutions of Greek states as his fundamental data. This is called inductive reasoning: observing as many examples as possible and then working out the underlying principles. Inductive reasoning is the foundation of the Western scientific method.

Outside of the empirical method, three characteristics stand out in Aristotle's thought: the schematization of knowledge, the four causes, and the ethical doctrine of the mean.

Perhaps the most fundamental aspect of Aristoteleanism is the classification of knowledge according the objects of that knowledge. For a long time, Greek philosophy dealt with questions of certainty; how could one be certain of knowledge? Suppose everything was an illusion? Aristotle resolved the question by categorising knowledge based on their objects and the relative certainty with which you could know those objects. Unlike Plato and Socrates, Aristotle did not demand certainty in everything. One cannot expect the same level of certainty in politics or ethics that one can demand in geometry or logic.

But Aristotle embraced the visible world of change and motion and sought all his life to describe the principles which bring about change and motion. He was the first major thinker to base his thought and science entirely on the idea that everything that moves or changes is caused to move or change by some other thing.

Aristotle works out an entire system of ethics based on the 'mean' to serve as a guideline to human behaviour. For example, courage. Courage is the opposite of cowardice. But, it is also the opposite of foolhardiness. Somewhere between foolhardiness and cowardice, that's where courage lies. What constitutes this 'mean' between the two terms varies from situation to situation. Therefore, every action needs to be judged according to all the relevant circumstances and situation. Aristotle called judging actions in this manner, 'equity', and equity is the foundation of modern law and justice.

Although the surviving works of Aristotle probably represent only a fragment of the whole, they include his investigations of an amazing range of subjects, from logic, philosophy, and ethics to physics, biology, psychology, politics' and rhetoric.

He died in 334.

❖❖❖

7

Neil Armstrong

(1930-)

On July 20, 1969, Neil Armstrong took a step out of the Apollo 11 lunar craft onto the moon. This "giant leap for mankind" made Armstrong the first man to walk on the moon, saying: "That's one small step for man, one giant leap for mankind."

Neil Armstrong was born on August 5, 1930, near Wapakoneta, Ohio.

He received a Bachelor of Science Degree in Aeronautical Engineering from Purdue University and a Master of Science in Aerospace Engineering from the University of Southern California. He holds honorary doctorates from a number of universities.

From 1949 to 1952, Armstrong was a naval aviator. He joined the National Advisory Committee for Aeronautics (NACA) in 1955. His first assignment was with the NACA Lewis Research Center (now NASA Glenn) in Cleveland. Over the next 17 years, he was an engineer, test pilot, astronaut and administrator for NACA and its successor agency, the National Aeronautics and Space Administration (NASA).

As a research pilot at NASA's Flight Research Center, Edwards, California, he was a project pilot on many pioneering high speed aircraft, including the well known, 4000-mph X-15.

Upon leaving military service, he became a test pilot. While thus serving, he transferred to astronaut status in 1962. He was assigned as command pilot for the Gemini 8 mission which was launched on March 16, 1966. During this flight, he and fellow astronaut David Scott successfully performed the first docking in space between two vehicles.

In July of 1969, Armstrong was the commander of Apollo 11, America's first attempt to land a manned vehicle on the Moon. On July 20, 1969 he and fellow astronaut Edwin Aldrin successfully touched down on the lunar surface. As Armstrong became the first person to touch the Moon's surface, he spoke the unforgettable phrase, "That's one small step for man; one giant leap for mankind." He and Aldrin explored the Moon's surface for nearly five hours.

Armstrong subsequently became Deputy Associate Administrator for Aeronautics, NASA Headquarters, Washington DC. In this position, he was responsible for the coordination and management of overall NASA research and technology work related to aeronautics.

He was Professor of Aerospace Engineering at the University of Cincinnati between 1971 and 1979. During the years 1982-1992, he was chairman of Computing Technologies for Aviation, Inc., Charlottesville, Va.

Armstrong is a Fellow of the Society of Experimental Test Pilots and the Royal Aeronautical Society; Honorary Fellow of the American Institute of Aeronautics and Astronautics, and the International Astronautics Federation. He is a member of the National Academy of Engineering and the Academy of the Kingdom of Morocco. He served as a member of the National Commission on Space (1985-1986), as Vice-Chairman of the Presidential Commission on the Space Shuttle Challenger Accident (1986), and as Chairman of the Presidential Advisory Committee for the Peace Corps (1971-1973).

Armstrong was awarded the Presidential Medal of Freedom in recognition of his accomplishments and his contributions to the space programme. He is the recipient of many special honours, including the Congressional Space Medal of Honor; the Explorers Club Medal; the Robert H. Goddard Memorial Trophy; the NASA Distinguished Service Medal; the Harmon International Aviation Trophy; the Royal Geographic Society's Gold Medal; the Federation Aeronautique Internationale's Gold Space Medal; the American Astronautical Society Flight Achievement Award; the Robert J. Collier Trophy; the AIAA Astronautics Award; the Octave Chanute Award; and the John J. Montgomery Award.

❖❖❖

8
Aryabhatta
(CE 476-550)

Aryabhatta suggested that the reason the stars and planets seem to move around Earth is that Earth is round and is in fact rotating on its axis—an idea literally a thousand years ahead of its time. He also maintained that the Moon and planets reflect light rather than generating it, and that the planets' orbits describe ellipses rather than circles. In addition, he provided an accurate explanation of the causes for solar and lunar eclipses.

Aryabhatta was born in. 476 in the region lying between Narmada and Godavari, which was known as Ashmaka, and is now identified with Maharashtra. Other traditions in India claim that he was from Kerala.

However, it is fairly certain that at some point, he went to Kusumapura (modern Patna) for higher studies, and that he lived here for some time. He lived there in the dying years of the Gupta empire, the time which is known as the Golden Age of India, when it was already under Hun attack in the Northeast, during the reign of Buddhagupta and some of the smaller kings before Vishnugupta.

Pataliputra, being the capital of the Gupta empire at the time of Aryabhatta, was the centre of a communications network which allowed learning from other parts of the world to reach it easily, and also allowed the mathematical and astronomical advances made by Aryabhatta and his school to reach across India and also eventually into the Islamic world.

The surviving text is Aryabhatta's masterpiece, *Aryabhattiya,* which is a small astronomical treatise written in 118 verses giving a summary of Hindu mathematics up to that time. Its mathematical section contains 33 verses giving 66 mathematical rules without proof. The *Aryabhattiya* contains an introduction of 10 verses, followed by a section on mathematics with, as we just mentioned, 33 verses, then a section of 25 verses on the reckoning of time and planetary models, with the final section of 50 verses being on the sphere and eclipses.

The consise but somewhat difficult-to-grasp *Aryabhattiya* also dealt with other aspects of mathematics and astronomical calculations, namely, geometry, plane trigonometry and spherical trigonometry, mensuration, square root, cube root, progression and celestial sphere. It also contains continued fractions, quadratic equations, sums of power series and a table of sines.

Aryabhatta gives a systematic treatment of the position of the planets in space. He gives the radius of the planetary orbits in terms of the radius of the Earth/Sun orbit as essentially their periods of rotation around the Sun. He believes that the Moon and planets shine by reflected sunlight, incredibly he believes that the orbits of the planets are ellipses. He correctly explains the causes of eclipses of the Sun and the Moon.

In his old age Aryabhatta also wrote another treatise, *Aryabhattasiddhanta*. It was a text-book for day-to-day astronomical calculations as well as a guide to determine auspicious times for various rituals. Even today Aryabhatta's astronomical data are used in preparing *panchangs* (Hindu calendars). It was in appreciation of his contributions to astronomy and mathematics that India's first satellite was named 'Aryabhatta'.

❖❖❖

9

Ashoka the Great

(304-232 BCE)

Ashoka was one of the most powerful kings of the Indian subcontinent. A ruler of the Mauryan Empire, his reign covered most of India, South Asia and beyond, stretching from present day Afghanistan and parts of Persia in the west, to Bengal and Assam in the east, and Mysore in the south. However, after the Battle of Kalinga, he turned into a Buddhist follower and started preaching the principles of Buddhism throughout the world. The Ashoka Pillar at Sarnath reminds us even today of his greatness. The Dharma Chakra, with three lions adorning it, has been adopted by the Indian Government as the device of its national Seal.

The great Indian emperor, Ashoka, was born in 265 B.C. The legend associated with the emperor goes that his birth had been predicted by Buddha, in the story of 'The Gift of Dust'.

Right from his childhood days Ashoka showed great promise in the field of weaponry skills as well as academics. He quickly grew into an excellent warrior general and an astute statesman. His command over the Mauryan army started growing day by day.

Ashoka's father Bindusura became seriously ill and was literally on his deathbed. A group of ministers, led by Radhagupta, called upon Ashoka to assume the crown. In the fight that followed his accession, Ashoka attacked Pataliputra, now Patna, and killed all his brothers, including Susima. After he became the King, he launched brutal assaults to expand his empire, which lasted for around eight years.

The battle of Kalinga (now Orissa) became a turning point in his life. The whole of the province was plundered and destroyed and thousands of people were killed. He could see nothing except burnt houses and scattered corpses. This was the first time in his life that he realised the consequences of wars and battles. It was during this time that he embraced Buddhism under the Brahmin Buddhist sages, Radhaswami and Manjushri. He started propagating its principles throughout the world, even as far as ancient Rome and Egypt.

Ashoka built thousands of stupas and viharas for Buddhist followers. One of his stupas, the Great Sanchi Stupa, has been declared as a World Heritage Site by UNECSO. The Ashoka Pillar at Sarnath has a four-lion capital, which was later adopted as the national emblem of the modern Indian republic.

Throughout his life, Ashoka followed the policy of non-violence. Even the slaughter of animals was abolished in his kingdom. He promoted the concept of vegetarianism. The caste system ceased to exist in his eyes and he treated all his subjects as equals. At the same time, each and every person was given the rights to freedom, tolerance and equality.

After ruling over the Indian subcontinent for a period of approximately 40 years, the Great Emperor Ashoka died in 232 BC.

❖❖❖

10

Sri Aurobindo

(1872-1950)

Sri Aurobindo was a great scholar, a revolutionary, mystical poet, philosopher, writer and yogi. After a short political career in which he became one of the leaders of the early movement for Indian independence from British rule, he turned to the exploration of the subtle realms of human existence and, as a consequence, developed a new spiritual path which he termed Integral Yoga.

Sri Aurobindo was born on 15 August 1872 in Kolkata, India, and named Arvinda Ackroyd Ghose. He studied in London and Cambridge, where he mastered Greek and Latin literature as well as the French, German and Italian languages.

In 1893 he returned to India and resolved to strive for Indian independence. He served the Maharaja of Baroda from 1893 to 1907, becoming successively professor of English, vice-principal at Baroda College, and finally principal of the National College of Calcutta.

The agitation against the partition (1905) of Bengal drew him into the nationalist movement, and for several years he acted as leader of a secret revolutionary organisation, becoming well known through his eloquent patriotic writings.

After the partition of Bengal, Aurobindo became a leader of a newly formed national party with the goal of home rule. When violence broke out in Bengal, he was arrested for sedition but was acquitted. He was again arrested and acquitted, but a third prosecution commenced while he was detained in prison. During his imprisonment he experienced visions that completely altered his outlook, turning him from politics to mysticism. In his major works, all written in English, he formulates the metaphysics and system of spiritual discipline that he called Integral Yoga (Purna Yoga). Rejecting the traditional ideal of world-renunciation and negation of physical existence, he based his philosophy on the principle of the descent of divine force and consciousness into both the individual and the universal processes of nature and history. He described evolution as the effect of progressively higher forces, of which the highest is the supramental force that initiates man's final transformation into a state of perfection.

Aurobindo taught that the material world should be transformed by making one's own life divine, and claimed that he had realised the 'Overmind' in 1926 and was thus able to bring divine consciousness to the task of human evolution. He retired into seclusion and from that time onward spoke to his disciples only through the Mother.

His writings include *The Yoga and Its Objects* and *Love and Death* (both 1921), *The Life Divine* (1949), *The Synthesis of Yoga* (1948), *Essays on the Gita* (1921–28, repr. 1950), *The Message and Mission of Indian Culture* and *The Mind of Light* (both 1953). During his lifetime he wrote a 23,000-line poem, *Savitri,* dealing with the struggle to unite divine consciousness with historical processes.

In 1914 he founded the magazine *Arya,* designed to promote his philosophical and religious teachings.

He retired from public life in 1910 and established an ashram at Pondicherry, where he lived until his death in 1950.

After his death the ashram continued under the guidance of Mira Richards (1878-1973), the wife of a French diplomat who had met Aurobindo in 1914 and embraced his philosophy. She became known as 'The Mother'. She conceived of the idea of Auroville as an ideal international urban centre.

❖❖❖

11

Johann Sebastian Bach

(1685-1750)

Johann Sebastian Bach was a German composer and organist whose sacred and secular works for choir, orchestra and solo instruments drew together the strands of the Baroque period and brought it to its ultimate maturity. He enriched the prevailing German style with a robust contrapuntal technique, an unrivalled control of harmonic and motivic organisation in composition for diverse instrumentation, and the adaptation of rhythms and textures from abroad, particularly Italy and France.

Johann Sebastian Bach was born on March 21, 1685, in Eisenach, Thuringia, Germany. Under his eldest brother, J.C. Bach, an organist and composer, he studied organ music as well as the construction and maintenance of the organ.

At the age of 14, he received a scholarship to the famous St. Michael's school in Luneburg, near Hamburg. There he lived and studied for two years. It was here that he sang a Capella at the boy's chorale. His studies included organ, harpsichord, and singing, theology, history and geography, and lessons of Latin, Italian, and French.

At the age of 17 he studied with Dietrich Buxtehude in the Northern city of Lubeck. Back in Arnstadt, he wrote 'Toccata and Fugue in D Minor' (1702), his first masterpiece; which stemmed from his bold organ improvisations.

Bach studied the orchestral music of Antonio Vivaldi and gained insight into his compositional language by arranging Vivaldi's concertos for organ. From the music of the Italians Antonio Vivaldi, Arcangelo Corelli, and Giuseppe Torelli; he adopted dramatic introductions and endings as well as vivacious rhythmical dynamism and elaborate harmonisation. He also performed the music of English, French, and Italian composers; motets of the Venetian school, and incorporated their rhythmical patterns and textural structures in the development of his own style.

Bach selected and instructed musicians for orchestras and choirs in Weimar and Leipzig. His work as a Cantor included teaching instrumental and vocal lessons to the church musicians and later to the musicians of the court orchestra.

Bach replaced his friend Georg Philipp Telemann as the director of the popular orchestra known as Collegium Musicum, from 1729 to 1750. It was a private secular music society that gave concert performances twice a week at the Zimmerman's Coffeehouse near the Leipzig market square. His exposure to such a secular public environment inspired him to compose numerous purely entertainment pieces for solo keyboard and several violin and harpsichord concertos.

Bach composed and played his *Mass in B Minor* to the monarch of Saxony and was appointed the Royal Court Composer of Saxony. King Frederick the Great invited him to Potsdam in 1747. There the king played his own theme for Bach and challenged the composer to improvise on it. Bach upgraded the king's theme to a more sophisticated melody which he titled *Musical Offering'* and later presented this composition to the king.

Bach wrote over eleven hundred music compositions in all genres. The complete list of Bach's works, BWV, has 1,127 compositions for voice, organ, harpsichord, violin, cello, flute, chamber music for small ensembles, orchestral music, concertos for violin and orchestra, and for keyboard and orchestra. His music became the essential part of the education for every musician.

Bach is by far the most performed and recorded composer in history. His *Das Wohltemperierte Clavier* (The well-tuned piano) is the definitive work for all students as well as concert musicians. His *Orgebuchlein* (The little organ book) is a staple in the repertoire of organists and pianists, and some pieces from it were arranged for ensembles.

In the last years of his life, Bach's creative energy was conserved for the highest flights of musical expression: the *Mass in b minor*, the *Canonic Variations*, the *Goldberg Variations*, and of course the *Musical Offering* displaying the art of canon. His last great work is the complete summary of all his skill in counterpoint and fugue; methods which he perfected, and beyond which no composer has ever been able to pass. This work is known to us as *Die Kunst der Fuge* (The Art of the Fugue, BWV 1080).

He died on 28 July, 1750 and was buried in St John's Cemetery.

❖❖❖

12

Samuel Barclay Beckett

(1906-1989)

Samuel Barclay Beckett was an Irish writer, dramatist and poet. He is one of the great names of Absurd Theatre with Eugéne Ionesco. He was awarded the Nobel Prize for Literature in 1969.

Samuel Beckett was born on Good Friday, April 13, 1906, near Dublin, Ireland.

He was sent off at the age of 14 to attend the same school which Oscar Wilde had attended. He was educated at the Portora Royal School and Trinity College, Dublin, where he took a B.A. degree in 1927, having specialised in French and Italian.

Beckett worked as a teacher in Belfast and lecturer in English at the École Normale Supérieure in Paris.

In 1931 he returned to Dublin and received his M.A. in 1931. He taught French at Trinity College until 1932, when he resigned to devote his time entirely to writing.

As a poet Beckett made his debut in 1930 with *Whoroscope,* a ninety-eight-line poem accompanied by seventeen footnotes. It was followed with a collection of essays, *Proust* (1931), and novel *More Pricks than Kicks* (1934).

Beckett's career as a novelist really began in 1938 with *Murphy* (1938; Eng. trans., 1957), which depicted the protagonist's inner struggle between his desires for his prostitute-mistress and for. total escape into the darkness of mind.

When World War II broke out, Beckett was in Ireland, but he hastened to Paris and joined a Resistance network. He worked as country labourer and wrote *Watt* (1953), his second novel, which was published in 1953 and was the last of his novels written originally in English. His other prose work includes *Stories and Texts for Nothing* (1955; Eng. trans., 1967), a collection of short stories.

After the war Beckett worked briefly with the Irish Red Cross in St. Lo in Normandy. Between 1946 and 1949 he produced the major prose narrative trilogy, *Molloy* (1951; Eng. trans., 1955), *Malone Dies* (1951; Eng. trans., 1956), and *The Unnameable* (1953; Eng. trans., 1958). The novels were written in French and subsequently translated into English with substantial changes. These books reflected his bitter realisation that there is no escape from illusions and from the Cartesian compulsion to think, to try to solve insoluble mysteries. He also wrote *Mercier et Camier*, a book of criticism.

Waiting for Godot (1952; Eng. trans., 1954) brought Beckett international fame and established him as one of the leading names of the theatre of the absurd.

Among his principal plays, pioneering works in the theater of the absurd, are *Endgame* (1957; Eng. trans., 1958), *Krapp's Last Tape* (1959), *Happy Days* (1961), *Play* (1964), *Not I* (1973), *That Time* (1976), and *Footfalls* (1976). *Endgame* developed further one of Beckett's central themes, men in mutual dependence. In *Krapp's Last Tape* Beckett returned to his native language.His last full-length novel was *Comment C'est* (1961, How It Is).

In the 1960s Beckett wrote for radio, theatre and television. In the 1970s appeared *Mirlitonnades* (1978), a collection of short poems, *Company* (1979) and *All Strange Away* (1979), which was performed in 1984 in New York. *Catastrophe* (1984) was written for Vaclav Havel and was about the interrogation of a dissident. In 1988, *Waiting for Godot* was produced at Lincoln Center. The 16-volume *Collected Works* were published in 1970.

Beckett's first play, *Eleutheria* (1947), was published for the first time in 1995, in an English translation His last book printed in his lifetime was *Stirring Still* (1989).

Beckett died, following respiratory problems, in a hospital on December 22, 1989.

❖❖❖

13

Kiran Bedi

(1949-)

Kiran Bedi is an Indian social activist and a retired Indian Police Service (IPS) officer. She became the first woman to join the Indian Police Service (IPS) in 1972. She has won many prestigious awards and for her effort to humanise the Tihar jail she was honoured with the 1994 Ramon Magsaysay Award.

Kiran Bedi born on 9 June 1949 in Amritsar.

She completed her schooling and graduation in Arts and earned a master's degree the following year in political science from Punjab University. She also acquired a law degree (LLB) from Delhi University. She was also awarded a Ph.D. in 1993 in Social Sciences by the Department of Social Sciences, the Indian Institute of Technology, New Delhi.

She began her career as a Lecturer in Political Science (1970-72) at Khalsa College for Women, Amritsar, India.

In the year 1972, she was selected for the Indian Police Service.

She has served creditably in a host of appointments ranging from Deputy Inspector General of Police, Mizoram, Advisor to the Lieutenant Governor of Chandigarh, Director General of Narcotics Control Bureau and many others.

She is well known for introducing a number of reforms during her stint as the Inspector General of Prisons of the Tihar Jail in New Delhi like detoxification programmes, yoga, meditation and redressal of prisoners' complaints.

She set up foundations like Navajyoti in 1988 and the India Vision Foundation in 1994 for improving the lot of drug addicts and the poor sections of society.

She has won a number of awards both in India and abroad. The prominent ones among include the President's Gallantry Award in 1979, Women of the Year Award (1980), the Asia Region Award for Drug Prevention and Control in 1991, the Magsaysay Award in 1994 for Government Service, the Mahila Shiromani Award (1995), Father Machismo Humanitarian Award (1995), Lion of the Year (1995), the Joseph Beuys Award in 1997, Pride of India (1999), the Mother Teresa Memorial National Award for Social Justice in 2005, and the Serge Soitiroff Memorial Award for drug abuse prevention, by the United Nations.

Kiran Bedi has had an illustrious career, earning widespread adulation for her no-nonsense attitude and devotion to work. She served as Police Advisor in the United Nations peacekeeping department and was honoured with the UN medal for outstanding service. She earned the nickname 'Crane Bedi' for towing away the then Indian Prime Minister Indira Gandhi's car for parking violation.

❖❖❖

14

Ludwig Van Beethoven

(1770-1827)

Ludwig van Beethoven was a German composer and pianist. He was a crucial figure in the transitional period between the Classical and Romantic eras in Western classical music, and remains one of the most acclaimed and influential composers of all time.

Ludwig van Beethoven was born on December 16, 1770 in Bonn, Germany.

At an early age, Beethoven took an interest in music, and his father, who taught him day and night, envisaged creating a new Mozart, a child prodigy.

On March 26, 1778, at the age of 7 1/2, Beethoven gave his first know public performance at Cologne. Soon Beethoven learned music, notably the organ and composition by renowned musicians, such as Gottlob Neefe. Apart from teaching him music, Neefe made the works of philosophers, ancient and modern, known to Beethoven.

In 1782, before the age of 12, Beethoven published his first work: nine variations, in C minor, for piano, on a march by Ernst Christoph Dressler. In June 1784, on Neefe's recommendations, Ludwig was appointed organist of the court of Maximilian Franz, Elector of Cologne. He was aged 14 years. Here he met people who were to remain friends for the rest of his life.

Prince Maximilian Franz was also aware of Beethoven's gift, and so he sent Beethoven to Vienna, in 1787, to meet Mozart and to further his musical education. But he returned to Bonn as his mother passed away on July 17, 1787.

In 1792, with another grant from the Prince Elector Beethoven went back to Vienna for two years, to pursue his musical education. He never went back to the town of his birth. Here, the young musician took lessons with Haydn, Albrechtsberger and Salieri. He captured the attention of Vienna with his virtuosity and his improvisations on piano.

In 1794, Beethoven composed his opus 1, three trios for piano. In 1795, he made his first public performance at Vienna whereby each musician was to play his own work.

In 1800, Beethoven organised a new concert at Vienna including the presentation of his first symphony. In 1802, he wrote a famous text which expressed his disgust at becoming deaf. But music made him carry on. Beethoven, knowing that his handicap was getting worse and worse, threw himself into his greatest works: exceptional sonatas for piano (*The Storm, opus 31*), the second and the third symphonies- *The Eroica* - and many more.

Beethoven wrote this third symphony in honour of Bonaparte, seen as the liberator of the people from the French Revolution. When the First Consul declared himself as the emperor, Beethoven became enraged and scowled out Bonaparte's name from the score.

As well as symphonies, Beethoven wrote extensively for the String Quartet. His later quartets also spread far into uncharted musical yet intimate territories. He wrote various other chamber works, several overtures, concertos, a Mass and one opera, Fidelio. He also wrote extensively for the piano with numerous sonatas and five concertos for that instrument, as well as some sonatas and a concerto for the violin.

Among Beethoven's many piano sonatas, is his *Moonlight* sonata with its famous first movement. Among his shorter works for piano is the ever popular *Fur Elise* and his *Minuet* in G, which also comes in this arrangement for flute and piano. Another piece available from the mfiles catalogue is the first movement of his first violin Sonata.

❖❖❖

15

Niels Henrik David Bohr

(1885-1962)

Niels Henrik David Bohr was a Danish physicist who made fundamental contributions to understanding atomic structure and quantum mechanics, for which he received the Nobel Prize in Physics in 1922.

Niels Henrik David Bohr was born in Copenhagen on October 7, 1885.

After matriculation at the Gammelholm Grammar School in 1903, he entered Copenhagen University where he came under Prof C. Christiansen, a highly endowed physicist, and took his Master's degree in Physics in 1909 and his Doctor's degree in 1911.

He then travelled to England on a study grant and worked under J.J. Thomson, who had discovered the electron 15 years earlier.

In 1912, he worked in Professor Rutherford's laboratory in Manchester. Based on Rutherford's theories, Bohr published his model of atomic structure in 1913, which is still commonly used and taught today as an educational simplification. He introduced the idea that an electron could drop from a higher-energy orbit to a lower one, emitting a photon (light quantum) of discrete energy. This became the basis for quantum theory.

In 1916, Bohr became a professor at the University of Copenhagen. In 1920, he became director of the newly constructed "Institute of Theoretical Physics" and was awarded the Nobel Prize in Physics in 1922 for his services in the investigation of the structure of atoms and of the radiation emanating from them. He later donated his gold Nobel medal to the Finnish war effort.

After 1930, he concentrated on research on the constitution of the atomic nuclei and of their transmutations and disintegrations.

In 1943, Bohr escaped to Sweden and then travelled to London. Then he and his son went to the United States, where both joined the government's team of physicists working on atomic bomb at Los Alamos. Bohr had qualms about the consequences of the bomb. He angered Winston Churchill by wanting to share information with the Soviet Union and supporting postwar arms control. He went on to organise the Atoms for Peace Conference in Geneva in 1955. After the war, he returned to Copenhagen, advocating for a peaceful use of nuclear energy. He received the first US "Atoms for Peace Award" in 1957.

Bohr died in Copenhagen in 1962. The element bohrium is named in his honor.

❖❖❖

16

Satyendra Nath Bose

(1894-1974)

Satyendra Nath Bose was an outstanding Indian physicist. He is known for his work in Quantum Physics. He is famous for "Bose-Einstein Theory" and a kind of particle in atom has been named after his name as Boson. He was honoured with Padma Bhushan.

Satyendranath began his education at an elementary school in Calcutta before entering the Hindu School in 1907. He completed his postgraduation in science from Calcutta in 1915.

Bose started his career in 1916 as a Lecturer in Physics in Calcutta University. He served here from 1916 to 1921.

He joined the newly established Dhaka University in 1921 as a Reader in the Department of Physics. In 1926, he became a Professor of Physics in Dhaka University.

Bose attracted the attention of Albert Einstein and other European physicists by publishing a paper in 1924 in which he was able to derive Max Planck's black body radiation law, but without using the classical electrodynamics as Planck himself had done. On the strength of this work Bose was able to get two years' study leave in Europe and during his visit he came into contact with many of the great physicists of the day, such as Louis de Broglie, Max Born and Einstein.

Bose sent his paper Planck's Law and the Hypothesis of Light Quanta (1924) to Einstein.

This paper was only four pages long but it was highly significant. The derivation of Planck's formula had not been to Planck's satisfaction, and Einstein too was unhappy with it. Now Bose was able to derive the formula for radiation from Boltzmann's statistics. The paper, and his method of deriving Planck's radiation formula, was enthusiastically endorsed by Einstein who saw at once that Bose had removed a major objection against light quanta. The paper was translated into German by Einstein and submitted with a strong recommendation to the Zeitschrift für Physik.

Bose published on statistical mechanics leading to the Einstein-Bose statistics. Dirac coined the term boson (thus honouring Bose) for particles obeying these statistics.

In 1945, he was appointed as Khaira Professor of Physics in Calcutta University. He retired from Calcutta University in 1956. The University honoured him on his retirement by appointing him as Emeritus Professor. Later he became the Vice Chancellor of the Viswabharati University.

It was not only for his research contributions that Bose is important, however, but also for his efforts to improve education in India that led to a much greater use of technology. His greatest honour was election to the Royal Society of London in 1958.

❖❖❖

17

Donald George Bradman

(1908-2001)

An Australian cricketer, Don Bradman is one of the greatest batsmen in the history of cricket with an impeccable record to his credit — an astonishing test batting average of 99.94. This has been one of the biggest achievements in the history of any sport till date.

Donald George Bradman was born in Cootamundra, New South Wales, on August 27, 1908.

He learned his cricket from his maternal uncles George and Richard Whatman. He honed his hand-eye coordination from a tender age. A local club team, Bowral Town, found themselves a man short when young Bradman was their scorer. He was invited to play and, batting at number ten, scored 37 not out. Soon afterwards he scored a remarkable 300 in one inning. This led to an invitation to audition at the Sydney cricket Ground (SCG). He played his first season in Shield cricket for New South Wales in 1927 and scored 118 in his first innings.

At the age of twenty he was selected to play for Australia against England, and he scored a century in his third test. Records continued to tumble. In a State match he scored a record 452, in record time for good measure.

In 1930, Bradman went to England for another eagerly awaited Ashes series. In his first Test innings of the tour he scored a memorable 236, including twenty-eight fours. News of the little

Australian genius had swept through Britain and as a result attendances swelled to double the usual when he was at the crease. The Don finished the tour with 974 runs from 7 innings, at an average of 139, including the then top Test score of 334.

The English were plotting the downfall of Bradman in a way that would shake the very nature of sportsmanship to its foundations. That summer, when England toured Australia, the captain of the side at the time, Douglas Jardine, devised what became known as 'The Bodyline Series'. The idea was for the bowler to aim a short-pitched ball at the chest, throat and head of the opposing batsman, with the majority of his fielders placed on the leg side. The anticipated result was one of the batsmen ending the dangerous ball away, giving a catch to one of the aforementioned fielders. At first Bradman struggled against this unique and often dangerous form of attack, with no helmets, chest guards or arm guards. With a range of improvised strokes he dominated the leg theory attack, but several of their players received blows to the head, back and chest. Eventually, because of Bradman's ability to deal with Bodyline and the Australian crowds' vehement disapproval, Jardine was forced to abandon it in favour of a more orthodox plan.

After achieving a merely excellent average in 1932 Don Bradman returned to amassing huge totals, especially against England but also West Indies and South Africa. In 1936 he was made captain of the national side. In that year England were 2-0 up in the five match series. Bradman came to the wicket and scored 270, the innings that many declare to be his best. That gave them the platform to go on and win the series 3-2.

After World War Two the Don was at it again, scoring 234 against England while injured. A year later he scored 187 not out, when Australia chased 400 runs in a day and won on a terrible batting surface.

Bradman played his last Test in England, 1948. He needed four runs to have an overall Test average of one hundred. It wasn't to be though – he was out second ball for zero, finishing with an incomparable average of 99.94. A year later he played his last game at the SCG (his favourite ground) and, fittingly, was given a huge standing ovation.

He was knighted in 1949. More than 50 years after his retirement as a Test player, he was conferred the title of the "greatest living Australian" in 2001, by the then Australian Prime Minister, John Howard. He was the only living Australian to have a museum dedicated to his life.

❖❖❖

18

Brahmagupta

(598 – 670)

Brahmagupta was one of the most significant mathematicians of ancient India. He introduced extremely influential concepts to basic mathematics, including the use of zero in mathematical calculations and the use of mathematics and algebra in describing and predicting astronomical events.

Brahmagupta was born in c. 598, perhaps in Ujjain which became a major astronomical and mathematical center.

Little is known of the life of this mathematician and astronomer who flourished 1,400 years ago. He is known mostly through his writings, which cover mathematical and astronomical topics and significantly combine the two.

Brahmagupta's first manuscript, the Brahma sphuta siddhanta, was a revision of an older astronomy book, the Brahmasiddanta (Doctrine of Brahma). It dealt with the position and motions of the planets and stars, the cycle of daylight and night, lunar and solar eclipses, the heliacal risings and settings of stars, planets, and moon. In it he discusses phases of the moon, planetary conjunctions and conjunctions between planets and stars. There is also a discussion of previous astronomical treatises, instruments and units of measure.

Brahmagupta's first manuscript calculated the length of the solar year at 365 days, 6 hours, 5 minutes, and 19 seconds, among the most accurate of early reckonings and remarkably close to the actual value of 365 days, 5 hours, 48 minutes, and about 45 seconds.

In the Khandakhadyaka, Brahmagupta revised his conclusion and went a small distance in the wrong direction, proposing a length of 365 days, 6 hours, 12 minutes, and 36 seconds, probably relying on the work of Aryabhatta in arriving at this figure — all remarkable estimates in an era that had no sophisticated telescopes or scientific instruments.

After his discussion of astronomy, Brahmagupta then turned to mathematics, discussing arithmetic and algebra. These ideas laid the foundation for much of the later development of mathematics in India. His directions for the multiplication of large numbers involve multiplying one number by each digit of the other in a manner close to what students are taught today, although the numbers are written out in a different configuration. A curious feature of Brahmagupta's treatise is that it is largely written in verse.

Brahmagupta also introduced new methods for solving quadratic equations that would be recognizable to modern students of mathematics. He devised formulas for calculating the area of a cyclic quadrilateral. His method is still known as Brahmagupta's theorem. He investigated various higher functions of algebra and geometry, in each case building on and refining the mathematical heritage of the ancient world.

Perhaps Brahmagupta's most important innovations, however, pertained to his treatment of the number zero. He was the first to propose rules for the behaviour of zero in common arithmetical equations, relating zero to positive and negative numbers (which he called fortunes and debts). He correctly stated that multiplying any number by zero yields a result of zero, but erred in attempting to define division by zero. Nevertheless, he is sometimes referred to as the "Father of Zero".

The real impact of Brahmagupta's discoveries was felt in the Islamic world, where King Khalif Abbasid al-Mansoor (712–775) ordered Brahmagupta's writings to be translated into Arabic in 771, and they had a major impact on subsequent writers in the Arab world, including al-Khwarizmi, the "father of algebra."

He died sometime in 670.

19

Louis Braille

(1809-1852)

Louis Braille invented "braille", a world wide system of embossed type used by blind and partially sighted people for reading and writing. It has been adapted to almost every known language, from Albanian to Zulu. He gave the gift of independence and the joy of reading to thousands of people around the world.

Louis Braille was born in the French town of Coupvray, near Paris on January 4, 1809.

Louis often played in his father's workshop, unaware of the dangers of the sharp tools his father used in his profession. While playing, he stabbed in his eye with an instrument used to punch holes in leather. The wound wasn't very serious, but it infected and spread out to the other eye. At the age of 4, he became completely blind.

But Louis was a very bright boy, and with help from his family, he was able to receive a very rich education. He went to a normal school, studying with kids who weren't blind. Despite his handicap, he was one of the best students of his class.

At the age of ten, Louis went to the Royal Institution for Blind Youth in Paris. The lessons were oral, but there were books available in a raised-print system, invented by Valentin Haüy, the founder of the Royal Institution for Blind Youth in Paris. His system wasn't very efficient, though: the books contained large, raised letters, which took up a lot of room, so the books were very large and heavy.

Louis got the idea for the braille alphabet from a French army captain, Charles Barbier. It was very annoying soldiers had to make light before they could read messages, because the enemy could easily spot the light source and use it as a target. So he invented a tactile alphabet, allowing soldiers who knew the code to read and write messages at night, without the need for light.

He later saw the usefulness of his invention for blind people, and he adapted his alphabet so it could be used by the blind. He used the spelling as a basis for the alphabet, instead of the phonetics Barbier used. He also replaced the Barbier's 12-dot cell by a 6-dot cell. Being fond of music, he also customised the Braille system so it could represent music.

In 1829 he published a book, named *Method of Writing Words, Music and Plain Song by Means of Dots, for Use by the Blind and Arranged by Them.*

Plagued by ill health, Louis died of tuberculosis on January 6, 1852. He was buried in The Pantheon in Paris, France.

Before his death, his system never really got accepted. But in the next years, people realised the simple but powerful system was the perfect means for blind to read. Braille was reintroduced in 1854, two years after Braille's death. Today, the Braille system is the standard reading system blind children learn.

❖❖❖

20

Pearl Sydenstricker Buck

(1892-1973)

Pearl Sydenstricker Buck was a prolific American sinologist and Pulitzer Prize-winning American writer, a humanitarian, a crusader for women's rights, editor of Asia magazine, and philanthropist, noted for her novels of life in China. In 1938, she became the first American woman to be awarded the Nobel Prize in Literature, for her rich and truly epic descriptions of peasant life in China and for her biographical masterpieces.

Pearl Comfort Sydenstricker was born on June 26, 1892, in Hillsboro, West Virginia. Her parents, near the end of a furlough in the United States; took her to China when she was three months old.

From childhood, Pearl spoke both English and Chinese. She was taught principally by her mother and by a Chinese tutor, Mr. Kung.

In 1910, Pearl enrolled in Randolph-Macon Woman's College, in Lynchburg, Virginia, from which she graduated in 1914. She returned to China shortly after graduation when she received word that her mother was gravely ill.

In 1915, she married John Lossing Buck in 1917, and immediately moved to Nanhsuchou (Nanxuzhou) in rural Anhwei (Anhui) province. In this poor community, she gathered the material that she would later use in *The Good Earth* and other stories of China.

From 1920 to 1933, Pearl and Lossing made their home in Nanking (Nanjing), on the campus of Nanking University, where both had teaching positions.

Pearl had begun to publish stories and essays in the 1920s, in magazines such as *Nation, The Chinese Recorder, Asia,* and *Atlantic Monthly*. Her first novel, *East Wind, West Wind,* was published by the John Day Company in 1930, followed by *The Good Earth* (1931), *Sons* (1932), and *A House Divided* (1935), together forming a trilogy on the saga of the family of Wang.

In 1931, John Day published *The Good Earth*. This won the Pulitzer Prize and the Howells Medal in 1935, and adapted as a major MGM film in 1937.

Her other novels were *The First Wife and Other Stories* (1933), *All Men are Brothers* (1933), *The Mother* (1934), and *This Proud Heart* (1938) followed by books of non-fiction. In 1938, she won the Nobel Prize in literature, the first American woman to do so.

The biographies of her mother and father, *The Exile* and *Fighting Angel,* were published in 1936 and later brought out together under the title of *The Spirit and the Flesh* (1944). *The Time Is Now,* a fictionalised account of the author's emotional experiences, although written much earlier, did not appear in print until 1967.

In 1934 Pearl moved permanently to the US where she was active in American civil rights and women's rights activities. She published essays in both *Crisis,* the journal of the NAACP, and *Opportunity,* the magazine of the Urban League.

In 1942, Pearl and Richard (her second husband) founded the East and West Association, dedicated to cultural exchange and understanding between Asia and the West.

In 1949, she established *Welcome House,* the first international, inter-racial adoption agency. In 1964, to provide support for Amerasian children who were not eligible for adoption, she established the Pearl S. Buck Foundation, which provides sponsorship funding for thousands of children in half-a-dozen Asian countries.

Pearl Buck died in March, 1973 and buried at Green Hills Farm.

❖❖❖

21
Gautama Buddha

(c. 560-480 B.C.)

The Buddha, the Enlightened One, was an Indian philosopher, religious teacher, and the historical founder of Buddhism. He is regarded variously as a human spiritual teacher or an omniscient, active deity.

Buddha was born approximately in 560 B.C. in Northern India near Kapilavastu. He was named Sarvaartha Siddha. His mother, Maya Devi, passed away on the seventh day after his birth. His father's second wife Gautami brought up the child, and hence, he was named Gautama.

When he was born, a renowned astrologer predicted that he would be either a great king or a great renunciant. His father got him married to Yasodhara, fearing that his son may become a recluse if he was left to himself. But Buddha did not feel that a married life was appropriate for him. He felt that man was bound by various attachments in worldly life. One night, he left the palace, giving up his wife and young son, Rahul.

From his childhood, Buddha could not bear the sight of anyone in pain. He was saddened at the sight of the old ill-treating the young, of men in authority harassing the people and the big fish swallowing the little ones.

One day, Gautama saw sheep being driven to be slaughtered at a yajna. On being told that the ceremonial killing of the lamb would bring great good to the ruler and the state, he said, "To kill so that you may live longer and with fuller joy is a reprehensible act. You have to sacrifice, not a bleating sheep, but your own animality, the bestial lust and greed, hate and malice. Sacrifice these and you earn the heaven of unflinching peace."

Buddha did not attach any importance to religious rituals. He felt that it was more important to ensure that the five sense organs were pure to begin with. He sought to find out why the mind gets disturbed. He was intrigued at the sight of a dead body. None of these natural happenings gave him peace of mind. He undertook many spiritual exercises to find out what transcended these natural phenomena. He approached many great elders, but none could give him satisfactory answers. Ultimately he reached Gaya, and sat under a banyan tree to meditate on the problems that worried him. Before he attained Nirvana, he summoned his stepbrother Ananda to his side and said: "My dear child! I came to the world to teach Truth. If anyone asks 'Where is God?' the answer is, 'He is everywhere.' Truth is God. Speak the Truth. Do not harm anyone. Recognise that the highest Dharma is non-violence (Ahimsa)."

Buddha added, "Today I have found the truth about life. What is it? The sanctification of the five senses is the way of Truth. If the senses are polluted, of what avail are spiritual exercises? When the water in a tank is polluted, all taps will only give polluted water. Your heart is the tank. Keep it pure through purity of vision, thought, speech and action."

Noticing the imminent passing of Buddha, Ananda started weeping, and the Enlightened One said to him, "Ananda! It was for realising this blissful state that I had striven all these years. Why do you shed tears at this moment? You are looking only at my earthly body. You cannot know the internal bliss I am experiencing at this moment. It was the mind that stood between me and Self-Realization. Today I am free from the hold of my mind. That is the cause of my bliss. When the mind is absent, there is bliss." This realisation culminated in a transcendental mystical experience, his own enlightenment. At this point he became the Buddha.

All his life, Buddha gave the concept of Nirvana unprecedented exposure to a large portion of the Eastern world with his achievement of and subsequent teachings about the state of enlightenment. Within the realm of Christianity, the historical Christ echoed the same teaching, though in a veiled form, by saying that the Kingdom of Heaven is within us.

Buddha's message spread to many countries like Tibet, China, Ceylon, Burma, Thailand and Japan. The story of the life of the Buddha was popularised in the West through the book *Siddhartha* by Herman Hesse. Within the last few decades, many movies have been made of the story. The movie, *The Razor's Edge,* touches upon the difficulties involved in treading the path of spiritual unfoldment leading to Nirvana.

❖❖❖

22

Julius Caesar

(102/100 BCE- 44 BCE)

Julius Caesar was a Roman general and statesman whose dictatorship was pivotal in Rome's transition from republic to empire.

Gaius Julius Caesar was born in Rome on 12 July, in either 102 or 100 BC.

In 86 B.C., Caesar was appointed flamen dialis with the help of his uncle by marriage, Gaius Marius. The position identified Caesar with extremist politics, committing him further to the radical side when he married Cornelia, daughter of Lucius Cornelius Cinna in 84 B.C.

In 82 B.C., Caesar was ordered to divorce his wife by Lucius Cornelius Sulla, an enemy of the radicals. Caesar refused and prudently left Rome for military service in Asia and Cilicia. He returned in 78 B.C. when Sulla died and began his political career as a prosecuting advocate. Caesar then travelled to Rhodes to study rhetoric and did not return to Rome until 73 B.C. During his journey to Rhodes, Caesar was captured by pirates. While in captivity, Caesar convinced his captors to raise his ransom, which increased his prestige. He then raised a naval force, overcame his captors, and had them crucified.

In 69 or 68 B.C., Caesar was elected quaestor and curule aedile in 65 B.C., pontifex maximus in 63 B.C., and a praetor in

62 B.C. By this time, he was making a name for himself as a political figure.

Caesar was made governor of Spain in 61 B.C. When he returned to Rome the next year, he joined forces with Crassus and Pompey and formed the first triumvirate. The alliance between Pompey and Ceasar was solidified further when Pompey married Julia, Caesar's only child.

In 58 B.C., Caesar was appointed governor of Roman Gaul. During the next eight years, he successfully conquered Gallic Gaul to the north.

Pompey's wife Julia died in 54 B.C., breaking the family ties between Pompey and Caesar. Pompey was appointed sole consul in 52 B.C. In 49 B.C., Caesar was instructed by the Senate to lay down his command. Caesar crossed the Rubicon, a small river separating Gaul from Italy, signifying the start of the Roman Civil War. Pompey fled and within three months, Caesar ruled all of Italy. He then took Spain and continued to pursue Pompey all the way to Egypt. In 48 B.C., Pompey was murdered by an officer of King Ptolemy. Caesar remained in Egypt throughout the winter and dallied with Queen Cleopatra.

In 48 B.C., Caesar assumed the title of dictator. He returned to Rome for a short time in 47 B.C. but then left for Africa to crush his opponents. He departed for Spain in 46 B.C. to put down resistance there.

In 45 B.C., Caesar returned to Rome to put his empire in order. The Romans began bestowing him with a great number of honours. Caesar could now wear purple coloured triumphal clothing, and a laurel crown. He was even named a Dictator for life. His statues were erected and placed in temples, equalling him to a God. He also began minting coins with his image on them. The Romans elected him consul for life. He was allowed to hold any office he wanted. He was granted legal immunity from prosecution. He had supreme command of all the legions. He now had the right to appoint half of the magistrates. A tribe was named after him. A temple and priesthood was established and dedicated to his family. The month of his birth was renamed

Julius and his date of birth was a national holiday. He established a 365-day calendar with a leap year every four years.

On March 15, 44 B.C., a day known as the *Ides of March,* Caesar entered the Senate House. An assassination plot had been hatched by a group of 60 senators, including Gaius Cassius and Marcus Junius Brutus. As Caesar entered the Senate, he was stabbed 23 times. Among the assassins, who were more than 30 in number, were Casca and Brutus. After Ceasar was assassinated, Rome experienced another 13 years of civil war

❖❖❖

23

Catherine the Great

(1729-1796)

The Russian empress Catherine II, known as Catherine the Great expanded the Russian Empire, improved administration, and energetically pursued the policy of Westernisation. Under her rule Russia grew strong and rivalled the great powers of Europe and Asia.

Catherine II was born as Sophia Augusta Frederica in the German city of Stettin, Prussia (now Szczecin, Poland), on April 21, 1729.

Catherine studied religion (Lutheranism), history, French, German, and music. When she was fifteen, she went to Russia at the invitation of Empress Elizabeth to meet the heir to the throne, the Grand Duke Peter, an immature and disagreeable youth of sixteen. She converted to the Russian Orthodox faith, and married Peter in 1745. The marriage turned out to be an unhappy one as there was little evidence of love or even affection.

However, her loveless marriage did not overshadow her intellectual and political interests. She was ambitious as well as intelligent and unlike her husband, she took care to demonstrate her dedication to Russia and the Russian Orthodox faith. This loyalty would earn her a rightful place on the throne and win support of the Russian people.

When Empress Elizabeth died on December 25, 1761, Peter was proclaimed Emperor Peter III, and Catherine became empress. Only a few months after coming to the throne, Peter had created many enemies within the government, the military, and the church. Soon there was a plot to overthrow him, place his seven-year-old son Paul on the throne, and name Catherine as regent until the boy was old enough to rule on his own. But those involved in the plot had underestimated Catherine's ambition.

On June 28, 1762, with the aid of her lover Gregory Orlov, she rallied the troops of St. Petersburg to her support and declared herself Catherine II, the sole ruler of Russia. She had Peter arrested and required him to abdicate. He was killed in a brawl with his captors.

During her reign she reduced the powers of the clergy, continued to preserve friendly relations with Prussia, France and Austria and, in 1764, she specified Poland's borders and installed one of her old lovers as king of Poland. She understood that Russia needed an extended period of peace in order for her to concentrate on domestic affairs. This peace could only be gained through cautious foreign policy. The able Count Nikita Panin, whom she placed in charge of foreign affairs, was well chosen to carry out such a policy.

By 1764 Catherine was greatly influenced by the ideas of the Enlightenment, and it was in the spirit of the Enlightenment that Catherine undertook her first major reform. She proposed a system providing equal protection under law for all persons. She also emphasized prevention of criminal acts rather than harsh punishment for them. She sent troops to help her former lover, Polish king Stanislaw (1677–1766), suppress a revolt that aimed at reducing Russia's influence in Poland. Soon Turkey and Austria joined in by supporting the revolution in Poland. Two years later, after lengthy negotiations, Catherine concluded peace talks with Turkey. From this Russia received its first foothold on the Black Sea coast. Russian merchant ships were allowed the right of sailing on the Black Sea and through the Dardanelles, a key waterway in Europe.

Much of Catherine's fame rests on what she accomplished during the dozen years following the Pugachev uprising. In 1786 she adopted a plan that would create a large-scale educational system. The arts and sciences also received much attention during her reign. Under her direction St. Petersburg was turned into one of the world's most dazzling capitals. Theater, music, and painting flourished with her encouragement.

She died of a stroke on November 6, 1796.

❖❖❖

24

Subrahmanyan Chandrasekhar

(1910-1995)

Subrahmanyan Chandrasekhar, a great Indian scientist of the 20th century, did commendable work in astrophysics, physics and applied mathematics. He was awarded the Nobel Prize in Physics in 1983.

Subrahmanyan Chandrasekhar was born on October 19, 1910 in Lahore.

Till the age of 12, he studied at home under his parents and private tutors.

In 1922, he attended the Hindu High School. He graduated from the Madras Presidency College in 1930. In July 1930, he was awarded a Government of India scholarship for graduate studies in Cambridge, England.

On the advice of Professor P. A. M. Dirac, he spent the third of his three undergraduate years at the Institut för Teoretisk Fysik in Copenhagen.

Subrahmanyan Chandrasekhar completed his Ph.D. degree at Cambridge in the summer of 1933. In October 1933, he was elected to a Prize Fellowship at Trinity College for the period 1933-37.

In 1936, while on a short visit to Harvard University, he was offered a position as a Research Associate at the University of

Chicago and remained there ever since.

Chandrasekhar is best known for his discovery of Chandrasekhar Limit which plays a crucial role in understanding the stellar evolution. If the mass of a star exceeded this limit, the star would not become a white dwarf. It would continue to collapse under the extreme pressure of gravitational forces. The formulation of the Chandrasekhar Limit led to the discovery of neutron stars and black holes. Depending on the mass there are three possible final stages of a star - white dwarf, neutron star and black hole.

He is also known for his theory of Brownian motion (1938-1943); the theory of the illumination and the polarisation of the sunlit sky (1943-1950); hydrodynamic and hydromagnetic stability, including the theory of the Rayleigh-Bernard convection (1952-1961); the equilibrium and the stability of ellipsoidal figures of equilibrium, in collaboration with Norman R. Lebovitz (1961-1968); the general theory of relativity and relativistic astrophysics (1962-1971); and the mathematical theory of black holes (1974-1983).

He was awarded (jointly with the nuclear astrophysicist W.A. Fowler) the Nobel Prize in Physics in 1983. He received many honours for his outstanding contributions: the Royal Society's Royal Medal of 1962 in recognition of his distinguished researches in mathematical physics, particularly those related to the stability of convective motions in fluids with and without magnetic fields; the Copley Medal of 1984 in recognition of his distinguished work on theoretical physics, including stellar structure, theory of radiation, hydrodynamic stability and relativity; the Bruce medal of the Astronomical Society of the Pacific; the Henry Draper medal of the National Academy of Sciences (United States), and the Gold Medal of the Royal Astronomical Society.

From 1952 until 1971 Chandrasekhar was editor of the *Astrophysical Journal*, originally a local University of Chicago publication, but later a national publication of the American

Astronomical Society, then a leading international journal. He retired in 1980 but continued to live in Chicago where he was made professor emeritus in 1985.

He died on August 21, 1995.

❖❖❖

25
Charlie Chaplin

(1889-1977)

Sir Charles Spencer Chaplin, Jr., better known as Charlie Chaplin, was an Academy Award-winning English comedy actor, filmmaker, composer and musician in the early to mid- "Classical Hollywood" era of American cinema.

Charlie Chaplin was born in East Street, Walworth, London on 16 April, 1889.

When he was nine years old, he toured with a stage company, the 8 Lancashire Lads, and he his first taste of stage life. He also met a young Stan Laurel as part of the troupe.

Charlie got his first chance to act in a legitimate stage show when he was about 14; he appeared as the page boy in *Sherlock Holmes* which starred William Gillette. He then embarked on a career as a comedian in vaudeville which took him to the United States as a featured player in the Fred Karno Repertoire Company. He was an immediate sensation especially in the more physical comedy sketches.

When the Fred Karno troupe returned to the United States in the fall of 1912, Charlie Chaplin was offered a motion picture contract with Mack Sennett's Keystone Film Company which came into effect with the completion of his vaudeville commitments in November 1913. He was an overnight success prompting other producers to start negotiations for his services. When his Sennett contract was up, he moved on to the Essanay Company (1915) for a great deal more money.

In 1916, Chaplin signed with the Mutual Film Corporation to make 12 2-reel comedies including *The Floorwalker, The Fireman, The Vagabond, One A.M., The Count, The Pawnshop, Behind the Screen, The Rin, Easy Street, The Cure, The Immigrant* and *The Adventurer.* When his contract expired in 1917, he became an independent producer. He began constructing his own studios in the heart of Hollywood.

Early in 1918, he entered into an agreement with First National Exhibitors' Circuit. His first film under this new deal was *A Dog's Life.* With the start of World War I, he made a film *The Bond* for the US government, in support of the Liberty Loan drive. And in 1918 he produced a comedy dealing with the war. *Shoulder Arms* was a huge box office success making Chaplin more popular than ever. *Sunnyside* and *A Day's Pleasure* soon followed in 1919. In 1919 he joined with Mary Pickford, Douglas Fairbanks and D.W. Griffith to found the United Artists Corporation.

Charlie completed his contract with First National in 1921 with the release of a 6-reel masterpiece. In *The Kid,* he introduced Jackie Coogan, one of the era's greatest child actors. Also released in 1921 was *The Idle Class,* in which he played two roles.

Charlie made eight feature-length pictures with United Artists: *A Woman of Paris* (1923) which he wrote, directed and produced, and appeared in a cameo role; *The Gold Rush* (1925); *The Circus* (1928); *City Lights* (1931); *Modern Times* (1936); *The Great Dictator* (1940), in which he played a dual role and talked on the screen for the first time; *Monsieur Verdoux* (1947) in which the public saw a new Chaplin, minus his traditional moustache, baggy trousers and wobbly cane; and *Limelight* (1952).

In 1957, Charlie Chaplin released his comedy *A King in New York* which he wrote, acted in and directed, and for which he composed the music. In 1966, he produced his last picture, *A Countess from Hong Kong* for Universal Pictures.

Charlie Chaplin also wrote at least four books, *My Trip Abroad, A Comedian Sees the World, My Autobiography,* and *My Life in*

Pictures. He was an accomplished self-taught musician, playing a number of instruments well including the violin and cello. And along with the music for all his films, Charlie composed a number of popular songs.

Charlie Chaplin died on Christmas day in 1977.

❖❖❖

26

Frederic Francois Chopin

(1810-1849)

Frederic-Francois Chopin is widely seen as the greatest of Polish composers for the piano, the instrument for which he wrote almost exclusively.

Frederic Francois Chopin was born in Zelazowa Wola, Poland on March 1, 1810.

He showed great admiration for the piano at a very young age, and he composed two *polonaises* (Polish dances) at the age of seven years. He also gave concert performances to impressed audiences. The prodigy was featured in the Warsaw newspapers, and 'little Chopin' became the attraction at receptions given in the aristocratic salons of the capital.

He began his studies with violinist Wojciech Zywny in 1816. He continued his studies at the Warsaw Conservatory, under the tutelage of Wilhelm Wurfel. From 1823 to 1826, Chopin attended the Warsaw Lyceum, where his father was a professor.

At the age of 15 years, he published his first work (*Rondo, op.1*). At 16, he began to study harmony, theory, figured bass and composition with Jozef Elsner, a Silesian composer who taught at the Conservatory.

In early 1829, Chopin performed in Vienna, where he was received with several optimistic reviews. The next year, he returned to his homeland and performed the premiere of his piano concerto in F minor, at the National Theatre on March 17.

Chopin decided to move to Paris, in order to eschew the volatile political situation back home. On the road, he learned that the Russians had captured Warsaw, and he composed the great "Revolutionary Etude" in reaction thereto. Once in Paris, he began working on his first ballade (*Op. 23*) and scherzo (*Op. 20*), as well as his first etudes (*Op. 10*). It is also at this time that he began his unfortunate struggle with tuberculosis.

In the he completed some of his most popular works and performed regular concerts, receiving fantastic reviews. However, he was not in favour of public performance; he therefore imposed a constant demand of himself as a composer and as a teacher. He was demanded in the Parisian salons, and he played less reluctantly under these circumstances.

By 1849 most of his major works were completed and Chopin concentrated on mazurkas and nocturnes. His last work was a mazurka, in F minor. He regarded the Romantic movement with indifference, if not distaste, and rarely associated himself with it directly. Even so, today Chopin's music is considered to be the paragon of the Romantic style.

On October 17, 1849, Chopin died of tuberculosis and he was buried at the Père Lachaise Cemetery in Paris. Polish soil was sprinkled over his tomb in France, as he had requested.

❖❖❖

27

Christopher Columbus

(1451-1506)

Christopher Columbus was a Genoese navigator and explorer whose transatlantic voyages opened the way for European exploration, exploitation, and colonisation of the Americas.

Christopher Columbus was born in Genoa, Italy in 1451. He helped his father with the weaving, but he always wanted to sail the seas.

He didn't get to go to school very much, but he learned to read and write Spanish during his travels. He taught himself Latin because all the geography books were written in Latin.

After he read *The Travels of Marco Polo,* he felt that he could reach the Indies by travelling west across the ocean instead of heading east over land. As a Christian he wanted to spread the story of Christ to the people of far-away lands. He also wanted wealth for himself and for Spain, and he wanted to be famous.

He tried for eight years to get King Ferdinand and Queen Isabella to supply him with ships and money. Finally they agreed. The contract between them made Columbus the "Admiral of the Seas" and made him the Viceroy and Governor of the new lands. He would also get an option to buy one-eighth of the interest in any commercial venture with the new lands and get one-eighth of the profits, but he made more demands.

Columbus left Spain on August 3, 1492 with three ships: the *Pinta*, the *Niña*, and the *Santa Maria*. He stopped at the Canary Islands and then reached an island in the Bahamas which he called San Salvador. He explored Cuba and Hispaniola. He then returned to Spain with not only examples of gold that he had found and descriptions of the lush landscape but also natives that had been forced to make the return voyage. He returned to Europe to spread the word, and was named "Admiral of the Ocean Seas" by Ferdinand and Isabella.

On his second voyage in 1493, Columbus arrived in the Lesser Antilles with 17 ships and 1,200 men. This time too he stocked up at the Canary Islands before he moved on. He named the Dominica in November 1943, landed at Santa Maria la Galante, then sailed past Les Saintes, and arrived at Guadeloupe. He then turned his course northwards, sighted and named Montserrat, Antigua, Redonda, Nevis, Saint Kitts, Sint Eustatius, Saba, Saint Martin, Saint Croix, and the Virgin Islands. In 1493, he landed at Puerto Rico. He then returned to Spain via Hispaniola, Cuba, Jamaica and Hispaniola again.

In 1498, Columbus made his third voyage with six ships to the New World. He then went to Porto Santo, Madeira, Canary Islands, Cape Verde, Trinidad and the Gulf of Paria. After exploring the mainland of South America, he set sail to Margarita Island from where he sailed to Tobago and Grenada. He returned to Hispaniola but his treatment of the Spaniards and native population was so bad that when he returned to Spain he was arrested.

Columbus was later released and sent on one final voyage in 1502, aiming to find a passage to the Indian Ocean. He explored Central America before returning to Hispaniola. He lost his ships in storms and was stranded on Jamaica until ships arrived to rescue him.

Columbus died in Spain on 20 May, 1506. The second Monday in October is celebrated as Columbus Day in the United States.

❖❖❖

28

Nicolaus Copernicus

(1473-1543)

Nicolaus Copernicus was the first astronomer to formulate a scientifically-based heliocentric cosmology that displaced the Earth from the centre of the universe. His epochal book, 'De revolutionibus orbium coelestium' (On the Revolutions of the Celestial Spheres), is often regarded as the starting point of modern astronomy and the defining epiphany that began the Scientific Revolution.

Nicolaus Copernicus was born on Feb. 19, 1473, in Thorn (Torun), Poland.

Copernicus first studied astronomy and astrology at the University of Krakow, then famous for its mathematics, philosophy, and astronomy curriculum. Then he went to Bologna to study further liberal arts (1496-1501), medicine at Padua, and law at the University of Ferrara, from which he emerged in 1503 with the doctorate in canon law.

Shortly afterward he returned to Poland and eventually settled permanently at the cathedral in Frauenberg (Frombork). He not only faithfully performed his ecclesiastical duties, but also practised medicine, wrote a treatise on monetary reform, and turned his attention to a subject in which he had long been interested—astronomy.

By May 1514 Copernicus had written and discreetly circulated in manuscript his *Commentariolus,* the first outline of those arguments eventually substantiated in *De revolutionibus orbium coelestium (On the Revolutions of the Heavenly Spheres,* 1543). He proposed that a rotating Earth revolving with the other planets about a stationary central Sun could account in a simpler way for the same observed phenomena of the daily rotation of the heavens, the annual movement of the Sun through the ecliptic, and the periodic retrograde motion of the planets. Although he realised that his theory implied an enormous increase in the size of the universe, he declined to pronounce it infinite. These aspects of the Copernican treatise do not mitigate the novelty or the impact of the final theory, or the author's firm conviction that his system was an accurate representation of physical reality. Rather, they indicate the scope of the work that lay ahead and that was effectively addressed in the next century when Kepler determined the ellipticity of planetary orbits, Galileo formulated his new concept of motion, and Newton espoused his theory of universal gravitation.

The enunciation of the heliocentric theory by Copernicus marked the beginning of the scientific revolution, and of a new view of a greatly enlarged universe. It was a shift away from the comfortable anthropocentrism of the ancient and medieval world. A scientific theory that reflected so profoundly on humanity was not welcomed by the church, and it was only after the publication (1540) of *Narratio prima (A First Account),* by an enthusiastic supporter named Rheticus, that the aged Copernicus agreed to commit to print the theory already outlined in 1514. An undocumented, but often repeated, story holds that Copernicus received a printed copy of his treatise on his deathbed.

He died on May 24, 1543.

❖❖❖

29

Confucius

(551–479 BC)

The Chinese teacher and philosopher Confucius was the founder of the humanistic school of philosophy known as the Ju or Confucianism, which taught the concepts of benevolence, ritual and propriety. His teachings and philosophy have deeply influenced Chinese, Korean, Japanese, Taiwanese and Vietnamese thought and life.

Confucius's birth date is given in early sources as either 551 or 552.

Confucius unquestionably belonged to the aristocratic class known as the shih who served as court officials, scholars, and teachers. Confucius's first occupation appears to have been as keeper of the Lu granary and later as supervisor of the fields. In 518 he served as tutor to one of the prominent clans of Lu, the Meng, who wished their sons to be educated in the *li*, or ritual. He journeyed to Loyang that year to instruct himself in the traditional Chou ritual. Here he met the famous Taoist teacher Lao Tzu, who reportedly bluntly rebuked him for his stuffiness and arrogance.

The nominal head of state in Lu at this time was a duke, but the actual power lay in the hands of three clans: the Meng, Shu, and Chi. The most powerful of the three was the Chi, which was frequently in conflict with the ducal house and the other clans. In 517 Duke Chao of Lu took prisoner the prime minister, Chi

P'ing-tzu, and was immediately attacked by the other two clans. The duke fled to the neighboring state of Chi, Confucius apparently felt a certain loyalty to the duke and fled with him.

Confucius eventually returned to Lu. For several years he spent most of his time studying and teaching. He gathered around him a large number of students instructing them in ritual, music, history, and poetry. He finally did obtain the post he wanted in 501, this time with the legitimate government of Lu. He first served as magistrate of the city of Chang-tu and later as minister of justice. He thwarted a plot by Chi to kidnap the Duke of Lu and was able to force Chi to restore the territory it had seized from Lu.

Confucius then decided to leave his home in Lu accompanied by several of his disciples and embark on a long journey throughout the eastern states of Wei, Sung, and Ch'en. He was received with great respect by the rulers of the states he visited, and he even seems to have received occasional emoluments. He spent much of his time developing and expounding his ideas on the art of government, as well as continuing his teaching. He acquired a large following, and the solidification of the Confucian school probably occurred during these years of exile. Much of his time was devoted to teaching, and he seems to have remained more or less aloof from political affairs.

Confucius has been considered responsible for editing and writing some of the most important works in the Chinese tradition. According to relatively early sources, he arranged the classical anthology of early Chinese poetry, the *Book of Odes,* into its present order. He is also credited with writing parts of the great divination classic, the *Book of Changes (I ching),* and the book of ritual, the *Records of Rites (Li chi),* the *Book of Music (Yüeh ching),* the *Spring and Autumn Annals (Ch'un ch'iu),* which is a chronological record of the reigns of the 12 dukes of Lu, beginning with the year 722 and ending in 479 B.C.

Confucius taught that the primary task of the ruler was to achieve the welfare and happiness of the people of his state. To accomplish this aim, the ruler had first to set a moral example by his own conduct, and this example would in turn influence the people's behavior. Confucius rejected the use of a rigid legal system and believed instead that moral custom and voluntary compliance were the best ways of maintaining order in society.

Confucius is the first Chinese thinker to introduce concepts that became fundamental not only to Confucian philosophy but to Chinese philosophy in general. The most important of these are *jen* (benevolence), *yi* (propriety), and *li* (ritual). Confucius believed that the *chün-tzu*, or "gentleman" must set the moral example for others in society to follow. He saw education as a process of constant self-improvement and held that its primary function was the training of noblemen. He saw public service as the natural consequence of education and sought to revitalize Chinese social institutions, including the family, school, community, state, and kingdom.

Confucius died in 479.

30

Dalai Lama

(1935-)

Tenzin Gyatso is the 14th Dalai Lama. He is the head of the Tibetan government-in-exile based in Dharamshala, India. He is a spiritual leader revered among Tibetans who traditionally believe him to be the reincarnation of his predecessors.

His Holiness the Fourteenth Dalai Lama, Tenzin Gyatso, was born on July 6, 1935 in a small village called Taktser in northeastern Tibet.

He was recognised, at the age of two, in accordance with Tibetan tradition, as an reincarnation of Avalokitesvara, the Buddha of Compassion.

He began his education at the age of six and completed the Doctorate of Buddhist Philosophy in 1959. He took the preliminary examinations at each of the three monastic universities: Drepung, Sera and Ganden.

On November 17, 1950, he was called upon to be head of the State and Government after some 80,000 Peoples Liberation Army soldiers invaded Tibet.

In 1954, he went to Beijing to hold peace talks with Mao Tse-ung and other Chinese leaders, including Chou En-lai and Deng Xiaoping.

In 1956, while in India to attend the 2500th Buddha Jayanti Anniversary, he held meetings with Prime Minister Nehru and Premier Chou about deteriorating conditions in Tibet. His efforts to bring about a peaceful solution to Sino-Tibetan conflict were thwarted by Bejing's ruthless policy in Eastern Tibet, which ignited a popular uprising and resistance. This resistance movement spread to other parts of the country.

On 10 March 1959 the Tibetan National Uprising was brutally crushed by the Chinese army. Dalai Lama, followed by 80,000 Tibetan refugees, escaped to India, where he was given asylum.. Since 1960, he has resided in Dharamsala, India, known as Little Lhasa, the seat of the Tibetan Government-in-exile.

In the early years of exile, he appealed to the United Nations on the question of Tibet, resulting in three resolutions adopted by the General Assembly (1959, 1961, 1965), calling on China to respect the human rights of Tibetans and their desire for self-determination.

With the newly constituted Tibetan Government-in-exile, the Dalai Lama saw that the Tibetan refugees were rehabilitated in agricultural settlements. Economic development was promoted and the creation of a Tibetan educational system was established to raise refugee children with full knowledge of their language, history, religion and culture. The Tibetan Institute of Performing Arts was established in 1959, while the Central Institute of Higher Tibetan Studies became a university for Tibetans in India. Over 200 monasteries have been re-established to preserve the vast corpus of Tibetan Buddhist teachings, the essence of the Tibetan way of life.

In 1963, he promulgated a democratic Constitution, based on Buddhist principles and the Universal Declaration of Human Rights as a model for a future free Tibet.

In Strasbourg, France, on 15 June 1988, he elaborated the Five-Point Peace Plan and proposed the creation of a self-governing democratic Tibet, in association with the People's Republic of China: (1) Transformation of Tibet into a zone of peace. (2) Abandonment of China's population transfer policy that threatens the very existence of the Tibetans as a people. (3)

Respect for the Tibetan people's fundamental human rights and democratic freedoms. (4) Restoration and protection of Tibet's natural environment and the abandonment of China's use of Tibet for the production of nuclear weapons and dumping of nuclear waste (5) Commencement of earnest negotiations on the future status of Tibet.

Since 1967, His Holiness initiated a series of journeys during which he met various leaders, among them being the late Pope Paul VI at the Vatican in 1973, Dr. Robert Runcie, Archbishop of Canterbury, leaders of the Roman Catholic and Jewish communities, and spoke at an interfaith service held in his honour by the World Congress of Faiths.

Since his first visit to the west in the early 1973, a number of western universities and institutions have conferred Peace Awards and honorary Doctorate Degrees in recognition of his distinguished writings on Buddhist philosophy and for his leadership in the solution of international conflicts, human rights issues and global environmental problems. He received the Raoul Wallenberg Congressional Human Rights Award in 1989 and the Nobel Peace Prize in 1989.

❖❖❖

31

Rene Descartes

(1595-1650)

Rene Descartes was a famous French mathematician, scientist and philosopher. His views about knowledge and certainty, as well as his views about the relationship between mind and body have been very influential over the last three centuries. He has been dubbed as the "Father of Modern Philosophy".

René Descartes was born on 31 March 1596 in La Haye (now Descartes),Touraine, France.

He was educated at the Jesuit college of La Flèche in Anjou between 1606 and 1614. He studied classics, logic and traditional Aristotelian philosophy. He also learnt mathematics from the books of Clavius.

He received a law degree from Poitiers, Paris, in 1616, then enlisted in the military school at Breda. In 1618 he started studying mathematics and mechanics under the Dutch scientist Isaac Beeckman. After two years in Holland he travelled through Europe.

In 1619 he joined the Bavarian army. He occupied his leisure with mathematical studies, and was accustomed to date the first ideas of his new philosophy and of his analytical geometry from three dreams which he experienced on the night of November 10, 1619, at Neuberg, when campaigning on the Danube. He regarded this as the critical day of his life, and one which determined his whole future.

From 1620 to 1628 Descartes travelled through Europe, spending time in Bohemia, Hungary, Germany, Holland, Venice and France.

By 1628 Descartes settled down in Holland. There for twenty years he lived, giving up all his time to philosophy and mathematics. Science, he says, may be compared to a tree; metaphysics is the root, physics is the trunk, and the three chief branches are mechanics, medicine, and morals, these forming the three applications of our knowledge, namely, to the external world, to the human body, and to the conduct of life.

Descartes began work on his first major treatise on physics, *Le Monde, ou Traité de la Lumière*. This work was near completion when news that Galileo was condemned to house arrest reached him. He, perhaps wisely, decided not to risk publication and the work was published, only in part, after his death.

His first substantial work was the *Regulae* or *Rules for the Direction of Mind* written in 1628-9 but not published until 1701. This work shows his interest in method that he shared with many sixteenth and seventeenth century scientists, mathematicians and philosophers.

Although he was adamant in not publishing *Le Monde*, he wrote a treatise on science under the title *Discours de la méthode pour bien conduire sa raison et chercher la vérité dans les sciences*. Three appendices to this work were *La Dioptrique*, *Les Météores*, and *La Géométrie*. The treatise was published at Leiden in 1637. *La Dioptrique* is a work on optics. His approach through experiment was an important contribution. *Les Météores* is a work on meteorology and is important in being the first work which attempts to put the study of weather on a scientific basis. *La Géométrie* is by far the most important part of this work.

Descartes's *Meditations on First Philosophy* was published in 1641, designed for the philosopher and for the theologian. The most comprehensive of his works, *Principia Philosophiae*, was published in Amsterdam in 1644. In four parts, it attempts to put the whole universe on a mathematical foundation reducing the study to one of mechanics.

In 1647 he received a pension from the French court in honour of his discoveries.

In 1649 Queen Christina of Sweden persuaded Descartes to go to Stockholm. After only a few months in the cold northern climate, walking to the palace for 5 o'clock every morning, he died of pneumonia at Stockholm on February 11, 1650.

❖❖❖

32

Dhyan Chand

(1905-1979)

Major Dhyan Chand Singh was a former Indian hockey player and Olympian. Regarded as the best hockey player ever, he mesmerised Adolf Hitler for his exploits in the sport. He was awarded the Padma Bhushan. He got the title "Chand" from his first coach, Pankaj Gupta, who predicted he would one day shine like a chand or moon.

Dhyan Chand was born on 29 August 1905, in Allahabad, U.P.

After an early education he joined the Indian Army at the age of 16, in 1922. He was a Sepoy of the 14 Punjab Regiment. His wizardry with the hockey stick caught the attention of his seniors and soon earned him a place in the Indian national team. He gained international attention when he toured New Zealand with the army team in 1926.

In a match in 1927 he exhibited his skills against the English hockey team, netting 36 of India's 72 goals in 10 matches, at the London Folkstone Festival.

In 1928 he was selected to represent the Indian hockey team in the 1928 Summer Olympics in Amsterdam, Netherlands. He helped India win the gold meda,l winning the finals against the Netherlands by a score of 3-0. He netted two of India's three goals. As a centre forward, Chand led a dominant Indian team to three Olympic Games, including Amsterdam (1928), Los Angeles (1932) and Berlin (1936).

On the field he was named the "Wizard of Hockey" for he exerted complete control on the ball. It appeared that the ball used to stick to his hockey stick while playing. So great was the magic of Dhyan Chand that the Tokyo officials broke his hockey stick to search for a magnet inside. On one occasion, a lady from the audience asked Dhyan Chand to play with her walking stick instead. He scored goals even with them! An artist in Vienna depicted him as having eight arms.

In the 1932 Summer Olympics held at Los Angeles, USA, the team under Lal Shah Bukhari defended their title winning the gold. The team routed the United States hockey team 24-1, a record that exists till today. Chand contributed eight of those goals, and along with his brother Roop Singh formed a formidable core of the team. That particular year, he had scored 133 goals out of India's 338.

During a 1935 tour of New Zealand and Australia, he scored 201 goals out of the team's tally of 584 in 43 matches. He came face to face with Don Bradman at Adelaide. After watching him in action, Bradman remarked, "He scores goals like runs in cricket".

Dhyan Chand captained the Indian team in 1936 Summer Olympics final. The match was attended by Adolf Hitler who left midway as he couldn't bear to see his "racially superior" team being demolished. Sensing something amiss, Chand was ordered to change his stick, but the flow of goals continued. India won the match 8-1, with Dhyan Chand scoring 3 goals. He had scored a total of 59 out of the team's tally of 175 that Olympics.

After World War II, he continued to play till the age of 42. In 1948 he retired from the sport. Residents of Vienna, Austria honoured him by setting up a statue of him with four hands and four sticks, depicting his control and mastery over the ball. One of his statues is near the India Gate, New Delhi while another has been erected in 2005 at Medak in Andhra Pradesh.

In 1956, he retired from the army with the rank of Major. The Government of India honoured him that year by conferring upon him the Padma Bhushan. However the Arjuna award for sports excellence was never awarded to him.

Chand however died penniless and uncared for in 1979 in a hospital, receiving a meagre pension.

Exactly a year after his death, the Indian Postal Service issued a commemorative stamp in his honour. The Dhyan Chand National Stadium in New Delhi is named in his honour. August 29, his birth date, is celebrated as the National Sports Day in India. To commemorate his memory, the Government of India has instituted the Dhyan Chand Award which is presented each year to those sportspersons who not only contribute through their performance but also contribute to the sport after their retirement.

❖❖❖

33

Charles Dickens

(1812-1870)

Charles Dickens, a English Victorian era author, wrote numerous highly acclaimed novels including his most autobiographical 'David Copperfield". As a prolific 19th Century author of short stories, plays, novellas, novels, fiction and non, during his lifetime Dickens became known the world over for his remarkable characters, his mastery of prose in the telling of their lives, and his depictions of the social classes, mores and values of his times.

Charles John Huffman Dickens was born in Portsmouth, Hampshire, England, on February 7, 1812.

His father who worked as a clerk for the Naval Pay office was imprisoned for debt when Dickens was young. Dickens went to work at a blacking warehouse, when he was twelve, and his brush with hard times and poverty affected him deeply. He later recounted these experiences in the semi-autobiographical novel *David Copperfield.* Similarly, the concern for social justice and reform surfaced later in his writings.

As a young boy, Dickens was greatly influenced by the stories his nursemaid used to tell him and by his many visits to the theatre. Additionally, he loved to read. He was able to leave the blacking factory after his father's release from prison, and he continued his education at the Wellington House Academy.

Although he had little formal schooling, he was able to teach himself shorthand and launch a career as a journalist.

At the age of sixteen, Dickens got a job as a court reporter, and shortly thereafter he joined the staff of *A Mirror of Parliament*, a newspaper that reported on the decisions of Parliament. During this time he continued to read voraciously at the British Library.

In 1833, his first story of many, "A Dinner at Poplar Walk", was published in the Monthly Magazine. He also had some sketches published in the *Morning Chronicle* which in 1834 he began reporting for and adopted the pseudonym 'Boz'.

Fast becoming disillusioned with politics, Dickens developed an interest in social reform and began contributing to the *True Sun*, a radical newspaper. He continued his journalistic work until the end of his life, editing *The Daily News, Household Words*, and *All the Year Round*. His connections to various magazines and newspapers as a political journalist gave him the opportunity to begin publishing his own fiction at the beginning of his career.

His first book, a collection of stories titled *Sketches by Boz*, was published in 1836, a fruitful year for him. He serialised *The Pickwick Papers*, a publishing phenomenon, published in monthly instalments and sold over forty thousand copies of each issue.

Oliver Twist and *Nicholas Nickleby* followed in monthly instalments, and both reflected his understanding of the lower classes as well as his comic genius. These were followed by *The Old Curiosity Shop* (1840-1841), *Barnaby Rudge* (1841, *A Christmas Carol* (1843), *The Chimes* (1844), *The Cricket on the Hearth* (1845), *The Battle of Life* (1846), and *The Haunted Man* 1848).

Further travels to the United States and Canada in 1842 led to his controversial *American Notes* (1842). *Martin Chuzzlewit* was first serialised in 1843. In 1844 he settled in Genoa bringing out *Pictures From Italy* (1846). *Dombey and Son* (1846) was followed by *David Copperfield* (1849).

He collaborated with Wilkie Collins on the drama No *Thoroughfare* (1867). Novels to follow were *Bleak House* (1852-1853), *Hard Times* (1854), and *Little Dorrit* (1855-1857).

In 1859 he founded his second weekly journal *All the Year Round,* the same year *A Tale of Two Cities* (1859) was first serialised. *Great Expectations* (1860-1861) was followed by *Our Mutual Friend* (1864-1865). Dickens published some of his best-known novels including *A Tale of Two Cities* and *Great Expectations* in his own weekly periodicals.

On June 9, 1870, Charles Dickens died and buried in Poet's Corner of Westminster Abbey.

Unfinished at his death, *The Mystery of Edwin Drood,* was published in 1870.

❖❖❖

34

Walt Disney

(1901-1966)

Walter Elias Disney was a multiple Academy Award-winning American film producer, director, screenwriter, voice actor, animator, innovator in animation and theme park design, entrepreneur and philanthropist. As the co-founder (with his brother Roy O. Disney) of Walt Disney Productions, Disney became one of the best-known motion picture producers in the world. The corporation he co-founded is now known as The Walt Disney Company.

Walt Disney was born in Chicago, Illinois, on December 5, 1901.

He became interested in drawing at an early age, selling his first sketches to neighbours when he was only seven years old. At McKinley High School in Chicago, he divided his attention between drawing and photography, contributing both to the school paper. At night he attended the Academy of Fine Arts.

In 1918, Walt joined the Red Cross and was sent overseas, where he spent a year driving an ambulance, covered with drawings and cartoons, and chauffeuring Red Cross officials..

After the war, Walt returned to Kansas City, where he began his career as an advertising cartoonist. Here, in 1920, he created and marketed his first original animated cartoons, and later perfected a new method for combining live-action and animation.

In 1923, he left for Hollywood with nothing but a few drawing materials, $40 in his pocket and a completed animated and live-action film. Together with his brother Roy Disney, Walt set up a workplace in their uncle's garage, borrowed some money, constructed a camera and started working. Soon, they received an order from New York for the first *Alice Comedy* featurette, and the brothers began their production operation in the rear of a Hollywood real estate office two blocks away.

Mickey Mouse was created in 1928, and his talents were first used in a silent cartoon entitled *Plane Crazy*. However, before the cartoon could be released, sound burst upon the motion picture screen. Thus Mickey made his screen debut in *Steamboat Willie*, the world's first fully-synchronised sound cartoon, which premiered at the Colony Theatre in New York on November 18, 1928. Technicolour was introduced to animation during the production of his *Silly Symphonies*. Walt Disney held the patent for Technicolour for two years, allowing him to make the only colour cartoons.

In 1932, the film entitled *Flowers and Trees* won Walt the first of his 32 personal Academy Awards. In 1937, he released *The Old Mill*, the first short subject to utilise the multiplane camera technique. On December 21 of that same year, *Snow White and the Seven Dwarfs*, the first full-length animated musical feature, premiered at the Carthay Circle Theatre in Los Angeles. During the next five years, Walt completed such other full-length animated classics as *Pinocchio*, *Fantasia*, *Dumbo* and *Bambi*.

In 1940, construction was completed on Disney's Burbank studio. The staff swelled to more than 1,000 artists, animators, story men and technicians.

Disney's 1945 feature, the musical *The Three Caballeros*, combined live action with the cartoon medium, a process he used successfully in *Song of the South* and *Mary Poppins*. In all, 81 features were released by the studio during his lifetime. His inquisitive mind and keen sense for education through entertainment resulted in the award-winning *True-Life Adventure* series. Through such films as *The Living Desert, The Vanishing Prairie, The African Lion,* and *White Wilderness,* he brought fascinating insights into the world of wild animals and taught the importance of conserving the nation's outdoor heritage.

Disneyland, launched in 1955 as a fabulous $17 million Magic Kingdom, soon increased its investment tenfold. By its third decade, more than 250 million people were entertained, including presidents, kings and queens, and royalty from all over the globe. The concept of amusement part has been one of the most successful projects in history.

A pioneer in the field of television programming, Walt began production in 1954, and was among the first to present full-colour programming with his *Wonderful World of Color* in 1961. *The Mickey Mouse Club* and *Zorro* were popular favourites in the 1950s.

In 1965, Walt Disney turned to improving the quality of urban life in America. He personally directed the design on an Experimental Prototype Community of Tomorrow, or EPCOT, Florida, planned as a living showcase for the creativity of American industry. Walt Disney World opened to the public on October 1, 1971. Epcot Center opened on October 1, 1982.

In 1966, Walt Disney established the California Institute of the Arts, a college level, professional school of all the creative and performing arts at Valencia, 32 miles northeast of downtown Los Angeles.

In his lifetime he won more than 30 Academy Awards, about 7 Emmy Awards, honorary degrees from various Universities such as Harvard University, University of Southern California, Yale and

UCLA etc., France's Legion of Honor and Officer D'Adademie, Presidential Medal of Freedom, Best Showman of the World from the National Academy of Theatre Association and many more.

Disney died on December 15, 1966.

❖❖❖

35

George Eastman

(1854-1932)

George Eastman was an American inventor. He founded the Eastman Kodak Co. and invented roll film which was also the basis for the invention of the motion picture film.

Eastman was born on July 12, 1854 in Waterville, New York.

After his education in the public schools of Rochester, New York, Eastman worked briefly for an insurance company and a bank.

He was the first American to improve photographic methods by coating glass plates with gelatine and silver bromide. In 1879 his coating machine was patented in England, and in 1880 he received an American patent for it. He sold his English patent and opened a shop to manufacture photographic plates in Rochester.

In 1880 he perfected a process of making dry plates for photography and organised the Eastman Dry Plate and Film Company for their manufacture.

On September 4, 1888 Eastman registered the trademark Kodak, and received a patent for his camera which used roll film. The first Kodak camera was a simple, hand-held box camera containing a 100-exposure roll of film that used paper negatives. Consumers sent the entire camera back to the manufacturer for developing, printing, and reloading when the film was used up: the company's slogan was "You press the button, we do the rest."

In 1889 Eastman introduced roll film on a transparent base, which has remained the standard for film.

In 1892 he reorganised the business as the Eastman Kodak Company. In 1900 he introduced the Brownie camera, intended for use by children and sold for one dollar. A pocket Kodak was marketed in 1897, a folding Kodak in 1898, non-curling film in 1903, and colour film in 1928.

In 1925, Eastman gave up the day-to-day management of Kodak, becoming Chairman of the Board. He thereafter concentrated on philanthropic activities.

Eastman's love of music led him to establish and support the Eastman School of Music, a theatre, and a symphony orchestra.

Eastman gave away half his fortune in 1924 to such beneficiaries as the University of Rochester (of which the Eastman School of Music is a part), the Massachusetts Institute of Technology in Boston, the Tuskegee Institute and the Hampton Institute. He was also one of the first owners to introduce profit sharing as an employee incentive.

Plagued by progressive disability resulting from a hardening of the cells in the lower spinal cord, Eastman grew depressed knowing he would likely be spending the rest of his life in a wheelchair. On March 14, 1932 Eastman took his own life at age 77, and was buried at Kodak Park in Rochester, New York.

His former home in Rochester, New York, was opened as the George Eastman House International Museum of Photography and Film in 1947. The Rochester Institute of Technology has a building dedicated to Mr. Eastman, in recognition of his support and substantial donations. On the 100th anniversary of his birth in 1954, he was honoured with a postage stamp from the United States Post Office.

36
Thomas Alva Edison

(1847-1931)

Thomas Edison, a Ohio-born inventor, created devices invented the electric light bulb, electric generator, phonograph, wireless telegraph, motion-picture projector, and alkaline, iron-nickel batteries that transformed society.

Thomas Alva Edison was born on February 11, 1847 in Milan, Ohio.

Edison entered school in Port Huron. Because of hearing problems, he had difficulty following the lessons and his school attendance became sporadic. Nevertheless, he became a voracious reader and at age 10, he set up a laboratory in his basement.

At age 12, Edison took a job as a train boy on the Grand Trunk Railway and established a new lab in an empty freight car. He also began printing a weekly newspaper, which he called the *Grand Trunk Herald.* While working for the railroad, he saved the life of a station official's child, who had fallen onto the tracks of an oncoming train. For his bravery, the boy's father taught Edison how to use the telegraph.

From 1862 to 1868, Edison worked as a roving telegrapher in the Midwest, the South, Canada, and New England. During this time, he began developing a telegraphic repeating instrument that made it possible to transmit messages automatically.

By 1869, Edison's inventions, including the duplex telegraph and message printer, were progressing so well, he left telegraphy and began full-time inventing and entrepreneurship.

Edison moved to New York City and within a year, he was able to open a workshop in Newark, New Jersey. He produced the Edison Universal Stock Printer, the automatic telegraph, the quadruplex, and other printing telegraphs, while working out of Newark. To reduce costs, he built a new laboratory and machine shop in Menlo Park, New Jersey in March, 1876. Edison achieved his greatest successes in this laboratory and he was dubbed the "Wizard of Menlo Park".

In 1877, Edison invented the carbon-button transmitter, still used in telephone speakers and microphones. In December of the same year, he unveiled the tinfoil phonograph. In the late 1870s, backed by leading financiers including J.P. Morgan and the Vanderbilts, he established the Edison Electric Light Company. In 1879, he publicly demonstrated his incandescent electric light bulb. In 1882, he supervised the installation of the first commercial, central power system in lower Manhattan. In 1883, one of his engineers, William J. Hammer, made a discovery which later led to the electron tube. The discovery was patented the "Edison effect".

In 1884, Edison began construction on a new laboratory and research facility in West Orange, New Jersey. During his time in West Orange, Edison produced the commercial phonograph, the Kinetoscope, the Edison storage battery, the electric pen, the mimeograph, and the microtasimeter. In 1913, he introduced the first talking moving pictures.

In 1915, he was appointed president of the U.S. Navy Consulting Board.

Thomas Alva Edison died in West Orange, New Jersey on October 18, 1931.

❖❖❖

37
Albert Einstein
(1879-1955)

The German-born American physicist Albert Einstein is best known for his theory of relativity. He was awarded the Nobel Prize in Physics in 1921 for his explanation of the Photoelectric Effect and for his research in Theoretical Physics.

Albert Einstein was born on March 14, 1879, in Ulm, Germany.

He attended a Catholic elementary school in Munich. At the age of 10, he began attending school at the Luitpold Gymnasium. The school's promotion of rote learning adversely affected his learning and hence much of his early study was independent. At age twelve, he learned of the Pythagorean Theorem, developed a method of proving it, and began to study in depth a booklet on Euclidean geometry. He mastered differential and integral calculus by age 16.

After a year spent in Italy, he entered a cantonal school in Aarau, Switzerland. He graduated from the Polytechnic at the age of 21.

Finding no teaching positions, he settled for positions of tutoring and performing calculations. In the meantime, he wrote a research article on capillarity and an important journal *Annalen der Physik* published it.

In 1901, Einstein worked at the Bern Patent Office, where he was to spend many years working efficiently to make time for his private research and calculations. He used tutoring as another source of income.

In late 1902, he completed another scientific paper that was published in *Annalen der Physik*. Within the next two years, he published two more papers that also dealt with thermodynamics. This thermodynamic work aided him with his work in the Patent Office.

Finally, in the year 1905, while working in a Swiss patent office, Einstein wrote four major papers proposing a "special theory of relativity," a groundbreaking notion which laid the foundation for much of modern physics theory. They are among his most revolutionary. He theorised that light should be thought of as consisting of particles. He found that the entropy of radiation is best described by the entropy of gas particles, and then he showed that the ratio of energy vs. frequency would equal Planck's constant.

Next, he applied his particle ideas to the phenomenon of the photoelectric effect. He showed that the higher the energy of incident light, the faster electrons would be ejected from a metal. Einstein was able to derive extremely simple photoelectric formula that transcended the current knowledge of his time on the subject. He asserted that space and time are not absolute, but the speed of light is. He investigated the thermal properties of light with a low radiation density and his observations laid the foundation of the photon theory of light.

Einstein soon became well known in the world of science. In 1909, after serving as a lecturer at the University of Bern, Einstein was called as an associate professor to the University of Zurich. Two years later he was appointed a full professor at the German University in Prague. Within another year and a half he became a full professor at the FIT. Finally, in 1914, after persuasions from Max Planck and Walter Nernst he accepted a lucrative research professorship at the University of Berlin, as well accepted their offer in 1914. He was elected to the Prussian Academy of Science and was assigned the directorship of the Kaiser Wilhelm Institute in Germany.

During the war years, Einstein expanded his theory of relativity to a general case. He developed a theory about the relationship of mass and energy. The formula, $e=mc^2$, is probably the most famous outcome from Einstein's special theory of relativity.

In 1920 Einstein was appointed to a lifelong honorary visiting professorship at the University of Leiden. By 1920 Einstein was internationally renowned; he won the Nobel Prize in 1921, not for relativity but for his 1905 work on the photoelectric effect.

However, he moved back to Princeton in 1933 upon the Nazi incursion. He joined the newly created Institute for Advanced Study. He lived there for the remainder of his life.

He gained numerous awards in recognition of his work, including the Copley Medal of the Royal Society of London in 1925, and the Franklin Medal of the Franklin Institute in 1935.

He died on April 18, 1955 at Princeton, New Jersey.

In 2000 *Time* magazine named him the leading figure of the 20th century.

❖❖❖

38

Thomas Stearns Eliot

(1888-1965)

American-English poet, playwright, literary critic, and a leader of the modernist movement in literature, Eliot was awarded the Nobel Prize for Literature in 1948. His most famous work is 'The Waste Land'.

Thomas Stearns Eliot was born 26 September 1888 in St. Louis, Missouri.

Eliot studied at Smith Academy in St. Louis and Milton Academy in Massachusetts. By 1906 he was a freshman at Harvard University. He studied philosophy at the Sorbonne in Paris, earning a B.A. and M.A. in English Literature. He also studied at Merton College, Oxford. Eliot also studied Sanskrit and Buddhism.

In 1914 he settled in England and worked as a schoolmaster and eventually met and became friends with many popular writers of the time including Ezra Pound.

Eliot taught for a year at Highgate Junior School in London, and then worked as a clerk at Lloyds Bank, wroting acticles for the monthly in-house magazine *Lloyds Bank Economic Review* on foreign currency movements. He also started editing the *Egoist* (1917–1919). Soon after he founded and edited the exclusive and influential literary journal Criterion. From 1919 onward he contributed regularly to the *Times Literary Supplement.*

In an early essay, 'Tradition and the Individual Talent' (1919), Eliot propounded the doctrine, that poetry should be impersonal and free itself from Romantic practices. In 1925, busy working with the publishing house Faber and Faber he also continued to write many poems and essays.

In 1927 he entered the Anglican Church and became a British subject.

Eliot's poetry from *Prufrock* (1917) to the *Four Quartets* (1943) reflects the development of a Christian writer: the early work, especially *The Waste Land* (1922), is essentially negative, the expression of that horror from which the search for a higher world arises. In *Ash Wednesday* (1930) and the *Four Quartets* this higher world becomes more visible. Collections of his poetry include; *Poems* (1920); *Poems 1909-1925* (1925); *Ash Wednesday* (1930); *Four Quartets* (1935–42); *On Poetry and Poets* (1957); *Collected Poems 1909-1962* (1963).

However, his dramas *Murder in the Cathedral* (1935) and *The Family Reunion* (1939) are more openly Christian apologies. He also wrote many plays including *The Rock: A Pageant Play* (1934); *Murder in the Cathedral* (1935); *The Family Reunion* (1939); *The Cocktail Party* (1950); *The Confidential Clerk* (1954); and *The Elder Statesman* (1959). The last five were published in one volume in 1962; Collected Poems 1909-62 appeared in 1963.

In his essays, especially the later ones, Eliot advocates a traditionalism in religion, society, and literature that seems at odds with his pioneer activity as a poet. In the essay 'Religion and Literature' (1935) Eliot stated that "literary criticism should be completed by criticism from a definite ethical and theological standpoint." With his collection of essays, *The Sacred Wood* (1920); *For Lancelot Andrewes* (1928); *Selected Essays, 1917–32* (1932); *The Use of Poetry and the Use of Criticism* (1933); *After Strange Gods* (1934); *Elizabethan Essays* (1934); *Essays Ancient and Modern* (1936); and *Notes towards a Definition of Culture* (1948) Eliot established his reputation as a literary critic..

Eliot's whimsical volume of children's verse, *Old Possum's Book of Practical Cats* (1939), was adapted into the long-running hit musical *Cats*.

In 1948 he received the Nobel Prize and the British Order of Merit, and the list of his honours continued to grow.

Eliot died on 4 January 1965, his ashes interred at the Parish Church of Saint Michael in East Coker, Somerset, England from whence his ancestors came. There is a memorial to Eliot in Poet's Corner in Westminster Abbey, London, England, his epitaph reading; "The communication of the dead is tongued with fire beyond the language of the living"

❖❖❖

39

Federico Fellini

(1920-1993)

Federico Fellini is considered one of the top film directors of all time, especially in Italy. His films highlighted artistic fantasy and desire and the line between reality and magic vanished in the scenes that he depicted in his movies, thereby creating the surreal imagery that many Italians, and in fact many playgoers around the world, have come to relish.

Fellini was born in Rimini in the resort city Adriatic on January 20, 1920.

He enrolled in law and then dropped out, took up a job as a crime reporter only to quit later. He settled down as a nomadic caricaturist and in 1939, was hired by the popular comic bi-weekly, *Marc Aurelio*. His strong points of sketching caricatures and cartoons and acting as a stand up comedian stood him in good stead when he entered cinema.

In 1941 he began working fervently as a scriptwriter and screenwriter: his name appears in the credits of films of the calibre of *Rome; Open City* (1945), *Paisan* (1946), *Senza pietà* (1948) and *Europa '51* (1952). The turning point in his film career took place in 1945, when he was asked to co-author the script of Roberto Rosellini's *Open City*.

Three years later, Fellini acted in Rosselini's *Ways of Love* where he played a tramp. His directorial debut was as co-director along with Alberto Lattuada of *Variety Lights* (1951). In *The White Sheik* (1952) which followed, written with Ennio Flaiano and Tullio Pinelli, he abandoned the neorealist tradition, depicting characters suspended between the fantastic and the ironic. He directed *I Vitteloni* which earned him the Silver Lion award at Venice as well as much public and critical acclaim.

The years to come brought one success after another: *La Strada* (1954) won him a well-deserved Oscar, as did another work, the intense *Nights of Cabiria* (1957. *La Strada* became a masterpiece and the crowning glory came when the movie won the Oscar prize for the best 'Foreign language film' category.

The hallmark works of his career were *La Dolce Vita* and *8 1/2* which he made in 1960 and 1963 respectively. Having given the world a taste of what he was capable of delivering, people eagerly awaited his next movie, *Federico Fellini 8 1/2*. The superb film won him his third Oscar and is widely considered his best film.

Fellini's first movie in colour was *Juliet of the Spirits*, which was released in 1965. For the first time, Fellini got more brickbats for a movie, than bouquets.

Satyricon is lauded by many as his perfect film. Later movies like *The Clowns*(1971), *Roma* (1972), and the little-known *Orchestral rehearsal* (1979) did include his central theme of fantasy and dreamlike characteristics, but it was beginning to get evident that his best was past him.

For Fellini the return to his native town of Rimini in *Amarcord* (1973) has palingenetic effects, and here again the director is at his best; another work whose mastery induces a sense of reverence is Fellini's *Fellini's Casanova* (1976), a dark, hypochondriacal work of extraordinary surrender.

Amarcord, which he made in 1974, was his best movie after *Satyricon* and it won him his fourth Oscar for 'Best Foreign Film.'

The menacing tale of *Orchestra rehearsal* (1979), the unnecessary journey into the subconscious of *City of women* (1980), the pretentious allusions of *And the ship sails on* (1983) all point to an inspiration block: Fellini sought refuge from this crisis in the placid anti-consumerist diatribe of *Ginger and Fred* (1985) and in the amusing, melancholic notes of *Fellini's intervista* (1987).

His final movie was made in 1990 and was titled *Voice of the Moon.*

He won an Oscar for 'Lifetime Achievement in Film making' in 1994.

He died of a stroke in August 1994 at the age of 73.

❖❖❖

40

Benjamin Franklin

(1706-1790)

Benjamin Franklin was one of the Founding Fathers of the United States of America. A noted polymath, Franklin was a leading author and printer, satirist, political theorist, politician, scientist, inventor, civic activist, statesman, and diplomat. He invented the lightning rod, bifocals, the Franklin stove, a carriage odometer, and the glass 'armonica'. As a diplomat during the American Revolution, he secured the French alliance that helped to make independence possible. He was a member of the committee that drafted the Declaration of Independence and was one of its signatories. He also signed the Constitution of the United States, and served as the new nation's ablest diplomat.

Benjamin Franklin was born in Boston on January 17, 1706.

Young Benjamin loved to read and was apprenticed to his brother James, a printer. After helping James compose pamphlets and set type which was grueling work, 12-year-old Benjamin would sell their products in the streets.

When he was 15 his brother started *The New England Courant,* the first newspaper in Boston carrying articles, opinion pieces written by James's friends, advertisements, and news of ship schedules.

Benjamin wanted to write for the paper too, but he knew that James would never let him. So he began writing letters at night and signing them with the name of a fictional widow, Silence Dogood. They were a smash hit, and everyone wanted to know who was the real "Silence Dogood."

James was thrown in jail for his views on smallpox and inoculation, and for making fun of the clergy. Benjamin was left to run the paper for several issues. Upon release from jail, James, instead of being grateful to Ben for keeping the paper going, kept harassing him and administering beatings from time to time. Ben could not take it. He went to Philadelphia and found work as an apprentice printer. He did so well that the governor of Pennsylvania promised to set him up in business for himself if young Franklin would just go to London to buy fonts and printing equipment. Ben obliged but the governor reneged on his promise and Ben was forced to spend several months in England doing print work.

Upon returning to Philadelphia, he went back to being a printer's helper. Then he borrowed some money and set himself up in the printing business. Soon he began getting the contract to do government jobs and started thriving in business.

In 1729, he bought a newspaper, the *Pennsylvania Gazette*. He not only printed the paper, but often contributed pieces to the paper under aliases. His newspaper soon became the most successful in the colonies. This newspaper, among other firsts, would print the first political cartoon, authored by Ben himself.

In 1733 he started publishing *Poor Richard's Almanack* under the guise of a man named Richard Saunders, a poor man who needed money to take care of his carping wife. What distinguished his almanac were his witty aphorisms and lively writing.

He helped launch projects to pave, clean and light

Philadelphia's streets Among his chief accomplishments in this era was helping to launch the Library Company in 1731; in 1743, the American Philosophical Society, the first learned society in America; and the Pennsylvania Hospital in 1751. In 1736, he organised Philadelphia's Union Fire Company, the first in the city. In 1752, he helped to found the Philadelphia Contribution for Insurance Against Loss by Fire.

By 1749 he retired from business and started concentrating on science, experiments, and inventions. In 1743, he had invented a heat-efficient stove, called the Franklin stove, to help warm houses efficiently. Among his other inventions are swim fins, the glass armonica (a musical instrument) and bifocals. In the early 1750's he turned to the study of electricity. His observations, including his kite experiment which verified the nature of electricity and lightning brought him international fame.

In 1757, he went to England to represent Pennsylvania in its fight with the descendants of the Penn family over who should represent the Colony. He remained in England to 1775, as a Colonial representative of Pennsylvania, Georgia, New Jersey and Massachusetts.

In 1765, Franklin was caught by surprise by America's overwhelming opposition to the Stamp Act. His testimony before Parliament helped persuade the members to repeal the law. He started working actively for Independence. Franklin was elected to the Second Continental Congress and worked on a committee of five that helped to draft the Declaration of Independence. Though much of the writing is Thomas Jefferson's, much of the contribution is Franklin's. In 1776 he signed the Declaration, and afterward sailed to France as an ambassador to the Court of Louis XVI.

When the government of France signed a Treaty of Alliance with the Americans in 1783, Franklin was on hand to sign the Treaty of Paris. He became President of the

Executive Council of Pennsylvania. He served as a delegate to the Constitutional Convention and signed the Constitution. One of his last public acts was writing an anti-slavery treatise in 1789.

Franklin died on April 17, 1790 at the age of 84.

❖❖❖

41

Sigmund Freud

(1856-1939)

Sigmund Freud was an Austrian psychiatrist who founded the psychoanalytic school of psychology. His work marked the beginning of a modern, dynamic psychology by providing the first well-organised explanation of the inner mental forces determining human behaviour.

Sigmund Freud was born on May 6, 1856, in Freiberg, Moravia (now Czech Republic). When he was four, the family moved to Vienna.

Freud attended the Sperl Gymnasium, a secondary school in Europe, in Leopoldstadt. He studied Greek and Latin, mathematics, history, and the natural sciences.

Freud enrolled in medical school in 1873 and received his doctor of medicine degree at the age of twenty-four. He spent three years as a resident physician in the famous Allgemeine Krankenhaus, a general hospital and the medical centre of Vienna. He spent five months in the psychiatry department headed by Theodor Meynert. He spent four months at the Salpêtrière clinic in Paris, studying under the neurologist Jean Martin Charcot. There the hypnotic treatment of women, who suffered from a medical state called 'hysteria', led him to take an interest in psychiatry.

Freud returned to Vienna, established himself in the private practice of neurology, and soon devoted his efforts to the treatment of hysterical patients with the help of hypnosis. His former tutor, Breuer, had with some success treated patients by encouraging them to 'talk out' their past under hypnosis. Together with Breuer he published *Studies on Hysteria* (1895).

At the age of thirty-nine Freud first used the term "psychoanalysis", and his major lifework was well under way. He began his own self-analysis which he pursued primarily by analysing his dreams. A major scientific result was *The Interpretation of Dreams* (1901). In this he analysed dreams in terms of unconscious desires and experiences.

By the turn of the century Freud had developed his therapeutic technique, dropping the use of hypnosis to the more effective and more widely applicable method of "free association".

Following his work on dreams, he wrote a series of papers in which he explored the influence of unconscious thought processes on various aspects of human behaviour.

In 1902 he was appointed Ausserordentlicher Professor, and in 1905 appeared *Three Essays on the Theory of Sexuality.* He described his highly debatable views concerning the early experiences of sexuality in *Three Essays on the Theory of Sexuality* (1905).

After 1902 Freud gathered a small group of interested colleagues on Wednesday evenings for presentation of psychoanalytic papers and discussion. This was the beginning of the psychoanalytic movement. Swiss psychiatrists Eugen Bleuler and Carl Jung formed a study group in Zurich in 1907, and the first International Psychoanalytic Congress was held in Salzburg in 1908.

He published findings on the importance of aggressive and sexual drives (*Beyond the Pleasure Principle,* 1920); developed a new theoretical framework to organise his new data on the structure of the mind (*The Ego and the Id,* 1923); and revised his theory of anxiety to show it as the signal of danger coming from unconscious fantasies, rather than the result of repressed sexual feelings (*Inhibitions, Symptoms and Anxiety,* 1926).

He published *Group Psychology and the Analysis of the Ego* (1921), *The Future of an Illusion* (1927), and *Civilisation and Its Discontents* (1929), *Jokes and Their Relation to the Unconscious* (1905), *Leonardo da Vinci and a Memory of His Childhood* (1910), *Psychopathology of Everyday Life* (1960), *Totem und Taboo* (1955), and *Beyond the Pleasure Principle* (1955). At the request of the League of Nations, Freud collaborated with Albert Einstein in writing *Why War?* (1933).

Freud's theories, including the concept of the Oedipus complex, have had an enormous influence on art, literature, and social thinking. He spent his last year in London, England, undergoing surgery. His last book, *Moses and Monotheism* (1939), was completed in England.

He died of throat cancer on September 23, 1939. His death was eased by euthanasia. Freud asked his physician to give him a lethal dose of morphine.

❖❖❖

42

Galileo Galilei

(1564-1642)

Galileo Galilei was a Tuscan physicist, mathematician, astronomer, and philosopher who pioneered "experimental scientific method" and was the first to use a refracting telescope to make important astronomical discoveries. He has been called the "father of modern observational astronomy", the "father of modern physics", the "father of science", and "the Father of Modern Science". His contributions to astronomy include the telescopic confirmation of the phases of Venus, the discovery of the four largest satellites of Jupiter, named the Galilean moons in his honour, and the observation and analysis of sunspots.

Galileo Galilei was born on February 15, 1564 in Pisa, Italy.

As a 10-year-old, he attended school at Vallembrosa. In 1581, he entered the University of Pisa. Since his study of medicine was not interesting to him, he began to study mathematics instead. Here he began his study of the pendulum. But because of Galileo's low grades, his father took him out of the university in 1585. However, it was not until 1602 that Galileo made his most notable discovery about the pendulum - the time in which a pendulum swings back and forth does not depend on the arc of the swing.

In 1592, Galileo was appointed professor of mathematics at the University of Padua. While teaching there, he frequently visited a place called the Arsenal, where Venetian ships were docked and loaded. Galileo had always been interested in mechanical devices. Naturally, he became fascinated by nautical technologies, such as the sector and shipbuilding. In 1593, he was presented with the problem involving the placement of oars in galleys. He treated the oar as a lever and correctly made the water the fulcrum. A year later, he patented a model for a pump. His pump was a device that raised water by using only one horse power.

Galileo invented many other mechanical devices, such as the hydrostatic balance. But perhaps his most famous invention was the telescope. He made a telescope in 1609, that could magnify objects twenty times. He was able to look at the moon, discover the four satellites of Jupiter and the stellar composition of the Milky Way, observe a supernova, verify the phases of Venus, and discover sunspots. His discoveries proved the Copernican system which states that the earth and other planets revolve around the sun, disproving the theory that the sun revolved around the earth.

In 1632 he published his *Dialogue Concerning the Two Chief World Systems,* a work that upheld the Copernican system rather than the Ptolematic system and marked a turning point in scientific and philosophical thought. His last book, *Dialogues Concerning Two New Sciences* (1638), contains most of his contributions to physics.

Galileo's belief in the Copernican system eventually got him into trouble with the Catholic Church. He was warned by the order of Pope Paul V, that he should not discuss or defend Copernican theories. In 1624, Galileo was assured by Pope Urban VIII that he could write about Copernican theory as long as he treated it as a mathematical proposition. However, with the printing of Galileo's book, *Dialogue Concerning the Two Chief World Systems,* he was called to Rome in 1633 to face the Inquisition again. He was found guilty of heresy for his *Dialogue,* and was sent to his home near Florence where he was to be under house arrest for the remainder of his life.

In 1638, the Inquisition allowed Galileo to move to his home in Florence, so that he could be closer to his doctors. By that time he was totally blind.

In 1642, Galileo died at his home outside Florence.

❖❖❖

43

Mohandas Karamchand Gandhi

(1869-1948)

Mohandas Karamchand Gandhi was an Indian revolutionary religious leader who used his religious power for political and social reform. Although he held no governmental office, he was the prime mover in the struggle for India's independence.

Mohandas Gandhi was born on October 2, 1869, in Porbandar, Gujarat.

Gandhi was educated in Gujarat and England, where he qualified as a barrister. He was called to the bar on June 10, 1891, and sailed for Bombay. He practised law in Rajkot and Bombay, then for a brief period served as lawyer for the prince of Porbandar.

In 1893 Gandhi accepted an offer from a firm of Muslims to represent them legally in Pretoria, capital of Transvaal in South Africa. While travelling in a first-class train compartment in Natal, he was asked by a white man to leave. He decided then to work to eradicate race prejudice. This cause kept him in South Africa until 1914. Shortly thereafter, he called his first meeting of Indians in Pretoria and attacked racial discrimination by whites. This launched his campaign for improved legal status for Indians in South Africa, who at that time suffered the same discrimination as blacks.

Gandhi began to do menial chores for unpaid boarders of the exterior castes and to encourage his wife to do the same. He decided to buy a farm in Natal and return to a simpler way of life. He began to fast. In 1906 he became celibate, and he extolled Brahmacharya (vow of celibacy) as a means of birth control and spiritual purity. He also began to live a life of voluntary poverty.

During this period Gandhi developed the concept of Satyagraha, or soul force. Gandhi wrote: "Satyagraha is not predominantly civil disobedience, but a quiet and irresistible pursuit of truth." Truth was throughout his life Gandhi's chief concern, as reflected in the subtitle of his Autobiography: *The Story of My Experiments with Truth.*

In 1907 Gandhi urged all Indians in South Africa to defy a law requiring registration and fingerprinting of all Indians. He was imprisoned for two months but released when he agreed to voluntary registration. During his second stay in jail he read Thoreau's essay *Civil Disobedience,* which left a deep impression on him. He was influenced also by his correspondence with Leo Tolstoy in 1909-1910 and by John Ruskin's *Unto This Last.*

Two of his final legal achievements in Africa were a law declaring Indian marriages (rather than only Christian) valid, and abolition of a tax on former indentured Indian labour.

Gandhi returned to India in 1915. Immediately he joined in the task of building the Indian National Congress as a mass movement. His simple style of a white loin-cloth, white shawl, and sandals appealed to rural masses who soon gave him the title "Mahatma".

In 1919 Gandhi persuaded the Congress to launch a Non-Cooperation Movement that soon attracted the support of the Muslim community. This movement snowballed into a country-wide agitation which took a violent turn with the Chauri Chaura incident (1922). So he suspended the movement and was imprisoned. He was released in February 1924.

The repressive Rowlatt Acts of 1919 caused Gandhi to call a general strike throughout the country, but he called it off when violence occurred against Englishmen. Following the Amritsar Massacre of some 400 Indians, Gandhi responded with non-cooperation with British courts, stores and schools. The government followed with the announcement of the Montagu-Chelmsford Reforms.

During the next five years Gandhi devoted himself to the constructive programme — social work aimed at uplift of the poor and building Muslim-Hindu unity. He urged Indians to spin their own clothing rather than buy British goods. Gandhi aimed at improving the status of "untouchables" or Harijans, as he termed them.

Following the Simon Commission (1927-30) and the Nehru Report (1928), he launched the Civil Disobedience Movement (1930-33) which began with the famous Dandi March and the Salt Satyagraha. A British law taxed all salt used by Indians, a severe hardship on the peasant. In 1930 Gandhi began his "salt march" to the sea, accompanied by thousand marchers to the coast, where he picked up a handful of salt in defiance of the government. This signalled a nationwide movement in which peasants produced salt illegally and Congress volunteers sold contraband salt in the cities. This movement was suspended for a while as Gandhi participated in the Round Table Conference (1931) in London. But as the conference failed to produce any satisfactory results, the agitation was resumed upon his return to India. This led to the announcement of the Communal Award (1932) by the British government which gave communal representation in provincial legislatures. Gandhi undertook a fast that led to the Poona Pact (1932) by which untouchable leaders renounced separate representation for remaining within the Hindu fold.

Gandhi devoted the years 1934 through 1939 to promotion of spinning, basic education, and Hindi as the national language. He worked closely with Jawaharlal Nehru and Sardar Vallabhbhai Patel in the Congress Working Committee. He severed formal links with the Congress in 1934 but remained its guiding light. He moved to his ashram in Wardha and concentrated on the constructive programme until 1940 when he briefly resumed leadership of the Congress at a time when India had been declared to be at war. This declaration, made in 1939, was opposed by the Congress, which offered to support the war effort provided it was given a firm guarantee of independence. The rejection of such promise by the colonial government led the Congress to launch a Quit India Movement (1942). This national movement was ruthlessly suppressed and Gandhi was kept in detention at the Aga Khan Palace until 1944.

Between 1944 and 1945 Gandhi engaged in prolonged dialogue with M. A. Jinnah, leader of the Muslim League, for a political settlement that could accommodate both the Congress and the League. These discussions proved fruitless and, as the end of British rule loomed, Gandhi became increasingly sidelined in the discussions about the post-independence shape of India.

Gandhi's last major act as a national political leader was to fast for peace amidst growing sectarian conflict between Hindus and Muslims. Twice he fasted in Calcutta (1946 and 1947) to protest against the religious killing that was taking place.

In March 1947 the last viceroy, Lord Mountbatten, arrived in India charged with taking Britain out of India by June 1948. The Congress party by this time had agreed to partition, since the only alternative appeared to be continuation of British rule.

After partition in August 1947, Gandhi returned to Delhi to help restore harmony among Hindus and Muslims. His activities had aroused much hostility among Hindu extremists.

On 30 January 1948, Nathuram Godse, who was the editor of Hindu Mahasabah extremist weekly, shot Gandhi at point blank range while he was on his way to the evening prayer meeting. Gandhi died instantly.

44

Bill Gates

(1955-)

William Henry "Bill" Gates is an American business magnate, philanthropist, author, and chairman of Microsoft, the software company he founded with Paul Allen. According to the Forbes magazine, he is the richest man in the world and has held the number one position for many years.

William Henry Gates III was born in Seattle, Washington on October 28, 1955.

Gates attended public elementary school and the private Lakeside School. There, he discovered his interest in software and began programming computers at age 13.

In 1973, Gates entered Harvard University as a freshman, where he met Steve Ballmer (now Microsoft's chief executive officer). While still a Harvard undergraduate, he wrote a version of the programming language BASIC for the MITS Altair microcomputer.

In his junior year, Gates left Harvard to devote his energies to Microsoft, a company he had begun in 1975 with his childhood friend Paul Allen. Guided by a belief that the computer would be a valuable tool on every office desktop and in every home, the pair planned to develop software for the newly emerging personal computer market.

In 1975, before graduation Gates left Harvard to form Microsoft with his childhood friend Paul Allen.

Bill Gate's company Microsoft became famous for their computer operating systems and killer business deals. For example, Bill Gates talked IBM into letting Microsoft retain the licensing rights to MS-DOS, an operating system that IBM needed for their new personal computer. Gates proceeded to make a fortune from the licensing of MS-DOS.

On November 10, 1983, at the Plaza Hotel in New York City, Microsoft Corporation formally announced Microsoft Windows, a next-generation operating system.

In 1999, Gates wrote *Business @ the Speed of Thought*, a book that shows how computer technology can solve business problems in fundamentally new ways. The book was published in 25 languages and is available in more than 60 countries. It has received wide critical acclaim, and was listed on the best-seller lists of the *New York Times*, *USA Today*, the *Wall Street Journal* and Amazon.com. His previous book, *The Road Ahead*, published in 1995, held the No. 1 spot on the *New York Times'* bestseller list for seven weeks. Gates has donated the proceeds of both books to non-profit organizations that support the use of technology in education and skills development

In addition to his love of computers and software, Gates is interested in biotechnology. He sits on the board of ICOS, a company that specialises in protein-based and small-molecule therapeutics, and he is an investor in a number of other biotechnology companies.

Philanthropy is also important to Gates. He and his wife, Melinda, have endowed a foundation with more than $21 billion to support philanthropic initiatives in the areas of global health and learning, with the hope that as we move into the 21st century, advances in these critical areas will be available for all people.

❖❖❖

45

Kahlil Gibran

(1883-1931)

Kahlil Gibran was a Lebanese-American philosophical essayist, novelist, mystical poet and artist. He is chiefly known for 'The Prophet', a series of philosophical essays written in English prose.

Gibran Kahlil Gibran was born in North Lebanon, on January 6, 1883.

In 1888 he learnt Arabic, Syriac, and Arithmetic in a village school. In 1844 he emigrated Boston, U.S.A. He joined a local school where his name was anglicised to Kahlil Gibran.

He then went to Beirut, Lebanon, in 1898 to attend Madrasat-al-Hikmah, a Maronite college where he studied Arabic literature and cofounded a literary magazine.

Gibran's artistic talents were recognized early and he was introduced to F. Holland Day, a photographer, who tutored him in art and literature. Day proclaimed him a "natural genius" and became his mentor. Through Day Gibran was given entrée to Boston society, where he acquired valuable contacts.

After Gibran's mother died when he was 20, his sister supported him while he established himself as a writer and painter. In 1903 Josephine Preston Peabody, a poetess and friend, arranged for an exhibition of his work at Wellesley College; in 1904 Gibran exhibited his work at Day's Boston studio. Here, Gibran met Mary Elizabeth Haskell, who became his patron and tutor in English for two decades, providing funds for him to study painting and drawing in Paris. Before going to France, he studied English literature with her and had an essay about music, *al-Musiqa* (1905), published by the Arabic immigrant press in New York City. It was followed by two collections of short stories and a novelette in 1912. After *Spirits Rebellious*, an Arabic poem, was published in 1908, Gibran was called a reformer and received widespread recognition in the Arabic world.

From 1908 to 1910 he studied art in Paris with August Rodin. In 1912 he settled in New York, where he devoted himself to writing and painting. His early works were written in Arabic. His *Broken Wings* (1912) was published in New York. His most respected Arabic poem is the *The Procession* (1919).

From 1918 he published mostly in English. His first work in English appeared in 1918 when *The Madman*, a slim volume of aphorism and parables written in biblical cadence somewhere between poetry and prose, was published by the American firm of Alfred A. Knopf. His style, a combination of beauty and spirituality, became known as 'Gibranism'.

In 1919 Knopf published *Gibran's Twenty Drawings*; in 1920 *The Forerunner* appeared. Each book sold a few hundred copies. *The Earth Gods* (1931) was a dialogue in free verse between three titans on the human destiny. In October 1923 *The Prophet* was published. It is his best-known work, a partly autobiographical book of 26 poetic essays, which has been translated into over 20 languages. The slim volume of parables, illustrated with Gibran's drawings, is one of America's all-time best selling books; its fame spreads by word of mouth.

Although in failing health, Gibran completed two more books in English - *Sand and Foam* (1926) and *Jesus, The Son of Man*

(1928). After his death earlier essays were compiled and published, and his Arabic work has been translated into many languages.

Gibran was 48 when he died in New York City on April 10, 1931, of cancer of the liver.

❖❖❖

46

Mikhail Sergenyevich Gorbachev

(1931-)

Mikhail Gorbachev is a former Soviet statesman and General Secretary of the Communist Party of the Soviet Union (1985-91) and President (1988-91). He was instrumental in ending the Cold War, and major reforms known as glasnost and perestroika. He won the Nobel Peace Prize in 1990.

Mikhail Gorbachev was born in the village of Privolnoe, near Stavropol, on March 2, 1931.

Gorbachev did not have an easy childhood. His father was in the army, and was twice wounded. Remaining in the Russian countryside, Gorbachev and his mother had to engage in back-breaking work in the fields. For two years Gorbachev received no schooling.

Exceptionally, when he was still a teenager, he was awarded the Order of Red Banner of Labour for heroic feats of work. He had assisted his father, a combine operator (who was given the Order of Lenin) in bringing in a record harvest in 1948.

In 1952 Gorbachev joined the Communist Party and began studies at the Moscow State University, where he graduated from the law division in 1955.

He returned to his native Stavropol and began a rapid rise through the Komsomol and party organisation. By 1966 he was party first secretary for Stavropol city, and in 1970 he became kraikom first secretary, with it a year later membership in the Central Committee of the CPSU.

In 1978, at the request of Brezhnez, Gorbachev went to Moscow as a party secretary responsible for agricultural administration. Despite problems with agriculture in the Soviet Union at this time, he gained a solid reputation as an energetic and informed politician.

He rose rapidly through the highest echelons of the Communist Party, adding to his secretaryship candidate membership of the Politburo in 1979 and full membership in 1980. When Leonid Brezhnev died in November 1982, Gorbachev's duties in the Party leadership team were extended by Brezhnev's successor, Yuri Andropov, who thought highly of the younger man. By the time of Chernenko's death, just thirteen months after he succeeded Andropov, Gorbachev called the Politburo together. The next day (March 11, 1985) he was unanimously elected Soviet leader by the Central Committee, following a unanimous vote in the Politburo.

From the outset of his leadership he was convinced of the need for change, involving economic reform, political liberalisation, ending the war in Afghanistan, and improving East-West relations. He began an energetic campaign against inefficiency and waste and indicated his intention to "shake up" lazy and ineffective workers in every area of Soviet life, including the party. He also revealed an unusual friendliness.

As Prime Minister Gorbachev also sought to establish better relations with the United States. When new tensions developed between the two powerful countries, the leaders agreed to hold a preliminary meeting at Reykjavik, Iceland, in 1986. But the clearest signs of improving Soviet-American relations came in 1988 when Gorbachev made a positive impression when he entered a crowd of spectators in New York City to shake hands with people. In May and June of the same year, President Reagan visited Moscow.

Within the Soviet Union, Gorbachev promoted great political changes. In 1989 he set up elections in which members of the Communist Party had to compete against opponents who were not party members. He called for an end to the special status of the Communist Party guaranteed by the Soviet Constitution. He also ended the Soviet military occupation of Afghanistan.

Soviet Union consisted of nearly one hundred different ethnic groups. Many of these ethnic groups began to call for outright independence. Both industrial and agricultural production were declining, and the old system, in which the economy ran under centralised control of the government, no longer seemed to work. While Gorbachev wrestled with these problems, Boris Yeltsin, once considered an ally, became the country's leading supporter of radical economic reform. Yeltsin formally left the Communist Party in 1990, something Gorbachev refused to do, and was elected president of the Russian Republic in June 1991.

In August 1991 a group of Communist Party conservatives captured Gorbachev while he was on vacation in the Crimea and moved to seize power. But Yeltsin, not Gorbachev, led the successful resistance to the coup, which collapsed within a few days. When Gorbachev returned to Moscow, he was overshadowed by Yeltsin.

By the end of 1991, the Soviet Union had fallen apart. The Ukraine and the Baltic states declared themselves as independent, and real power began to shift towards the leaders of those regions, among them Yeltsin. Gorbachev formally resigned his remaining political office in 1991.

On May 25, 2000, Gorbachev registered his Russian Social Democratic Party, saying he wanted to support liberal ideas. The party's registration by the Justice Ministry paved the way for it to contest future polls.

❖❖❖

47

Steffi Graf

(1969-)

Stefanie Maria Graf is a former World No. 1 ranked female tennis player from Germany. In December 1999, Graf was named the greatest female tennis player of the 20th century by a panel of experts assembled by the Associated Press. When she chose to retire in 1999 she had an astonishing 107 career singles titles and 22 Grand Slam singles titles. She also became one of only five players in the history of the game to win tennis' Grand Slam, which she accomplished in 1988 by winning the four major tournaments all in one calendar year.

Steffi Graf was born on June 14, 1969 in Mannheim, Baden-Württemberg, West Germany.

As a child, Steffi was introduced to the game and coached by her father Peter. One of her first coaches was Boris Breskvar, a Slovenian tennis coach, who taught in Germany. As a young tennis player, Steffi won numerous juniors tournaments.

In 1982, at the age of 12, she won the European under 12 and 18 championships. She became a pro at the age of 13! She then went on to play in her first professional tournament in October of that same year. She played in her first professional tournament in Filderstadt, Germany, where she lost 4-6, 0-6. In the next year, when she played full time on the professional circuit, she began the season ranked 124th in the world and steadily improved, and was 6th in 1985.

In 1984, Steffi represented West Germany at the Olympics in Los Angeles in the tennis demonstrations and won the gold medal. It was then in 1986, she won her first tournament at Hilton Head, South Carolina, and then several more. She ended the year ranked 3rd in the world. In 1987, she starting by playing her way into the finals at Wimbledon, where she lost to world #1 Martina Navratilova and won several tournaments, including the 1987 French Open.

Soon Graf attained the number one ranking with the Women's International Tennis Association in 1987 and effectively moved past Chris Evert and Martina Navratilova,

In 1988, she started out by winning the Australian Open, Wimbledon, French Open, the Gold Medal at the Olympic Games in Seoul, and lastly the U.S Open, becoming the only player to win a "Golden Slam", all four Grand Slams in the same year, in addition to winning the Gold Medal at the Olympics, in addition winning the Bronze medal in doubles tennis as well.

She continued her dominance, winning 17 more Grand Slams and becoming a finalist in 7 more Grand Slam finals. She dominated women's tennis for over a decade. She was ranked number 1 for a total of 377 weeks including a record 186 consecutive weeks. She also won 107 singles and 11 doubles titles in her career.

Tennis writer Steve Flink, in his book, *The Greatest Tennis Matches of the Twentieth Century,* named her as the best female player of the 20th century.

She then retired in 1999, after winning her 6th French Open Championship. She was inducted into the International Tennis Hall of Fame in 2004.

❖❖❖

48

Otto Hahn

(1879–1968)

Otto Hahn was a German chemist and Nobel laureate who pioneered the fields of radioactivity and radiochemistry. He was a joint discoverer of nuclear fission. He is regarded as "the father of nuclear chemistry" and the "founder of the atomic age".

Otto Hahn was born in Frankfurt , Germany, on March 8, 1879.

After leaving school in Frankfurt, he went to Marburg University with the intention of entering the chemical industry. Research on bromine derivatives of isoeugenol led to a doctorate in 1901, and after a year's military service he returned to Marburg to continue his research. He worked at the Chemical Institute at Marburg for three years.

In 1904 he studied abroad, first with William Ramsay in London and then in 1905 at McGill University, Canada, with Ernest Rutherford. Here again success came quickly, and within a year he had recognised two other radioactive species, which he called thorium-C and radioactinium.

Hahn returned to Germany in 1907, where he took up an appointment at the University of Berlin, being made professor of chemistry in 1910. Here he discovered mesothorium, studied beta emissions, and recognised the phenomenon known as radioactive recoil.

At the end of 1907, Lise Meitner came to Berlin from Vienna, and the two began more than 30 years' collaboration. Their joint work embraced investigations on beta-rays and the use of the radioactive recoil to obtain new radioactive transformation products.

Between 1914 and 1918, Hahn served in World War I, but he resumed his research with Professor Meitner in 1918. A study of the radioactive precursors of actinium led to the discovery of the element protoactinium. He further discovered uranium Z, the first case of a nuclear isomerism of radioactive kinds of atoms. He also collaborated with Meitner and Fritz Strassmann on the processes if irradiating uranium and thorium with neutrons.

He went on to define, in 1921, the phenomenon of nuclear isomerism. This arises when nuclei with different radioactive properties turn out to be identical in atomic number and mass.

He joined the Kaiser Wilhelm Institute of Chemistry where he served as director from 1928 to 1945.

Hahn had trained as an organic chemist and had really gone to London to learn English in order to prepare himself for an industrial career. Ramsay had however asked him to separate radium from some radioactive material he had recently acquired from Ceylon. In so doing Hahn found a new material, a highly active form of thorium which he named 'radiothorium'. So impressed was Ramsay with this work that he wrote to Emil Fischer in Berlin suggesting that he employ Hahn after he had acquired more experience of radioactivity with Rutherford at McGill.

Hahn and Meitner also worked together on the discovery of an artificially active uranium isotope, which represents the basic substance of the elements neptunium and plutonium, first revealed later in America. But his most spectacular discovery came at the end of 1938 when, while working jointly with Strassmann, Hahn discovered the fission of uranium. This discovery earned Hahn the Nobel Prize in Chemistry in 1944, and led directly to the development of the atomic bomb.

In 1912, Hahn became scientific member of the Kaiser Wilhelm Institute for Chemistry and was Director of the Institute until it was taken into Allied custody following World War II. He, along with other key members of Germany's atomic bomb project were captured by the Allies and interned at Farm Hall, England.

Hahn died on July 28, 1968.

Germany's first nuclear vessel was appropriately named Otto Hahn.

❖❖❖

49

Dag Hammarskjold

(1905-1961)

Dag Hammarskjöld was a Swedish diplomat, author and statesman. He served as secretary general of the United Nations (1953-61. He was influential in the resolution of the Suez Canal crisis and initiated peace moves in the Middle East. He was was posthumously awarded the Nobel Peace Prize (1961).

Dag Hammarskjöld, the son of Hjalmar Hammarskjöld, prime minister of Sweden, was born on July 19, 1905 in Jönköping in south-central Sweden.

He took a degree in the humanities from Uppsala University. A talented linguist he spoke several languages including English, French and German. He took further degrees in economics (1928) and law (1930) and taught in 1933 began teaching at the University of Stockholm.

In 1930 Hammarskjöld was appointed secretary of the Royal Commission on Unemployment. He served next as secretary of the Central Bank. His economic expertise brought him the high post of undersecretary in the Ministry of Finance at the age of 31. Five years later he was named chairman of the Central Bank and also assumed the duties of commissioner and assistant undersecretary in the State Financial Office.

In 1946 he transferred to the Ministry of Foreign Affairs as an economic adviser. He became head of the Risbank. He drafted the legislation that introduced the Welfare State in Sweden. He was credited with being the first to use the term the "planned economy". The next year he served as Swedish delegate to the Paris conference on economic recovery and later was responsible for Sweden's role in the Marshall Plan. He helped in establishing the Organization for European Economic Cooperation (OEEC), serving as vice-chairman of its executive committee.

In 1949 he was appointed undersecretary in the Ministry of Foreign Affairs. He served as vice-chairman of the Swedish delegation to the General Assembly of the UN in 1952. The following year he became chairman of the delegation.

In March 1953 Hammarskjöld received the recommendation of the Security Council to replace Trygve Lie as UN secretary general, and on April 7 the General Assembly adopted the recommendation. He took office 12 days later.

During his initial year at the UN, he was involved in negotiating the release of American soldiers captured by the Chinese in the Korean War. He sought to streamline the operations of the Secretariat and to reduce the political interference of member states in Secretariat administration.

He was also involved in what he called "preventive diplomacy". This became even more apparent in the 1956 Middle East crisis, and the disputes in Palestine, Vietnam and Egypt. During the Suez Canal Crisis he managed to persuade the United Nations Security Council to condemn the actions of Israel, France and Britain. After the nationalisation of the Suez Canal in late 1956 and the subsequent military invasion of Egypt by Israel, France, and England, he led in getting these forces removed and the canal reopened. A crucial factor was the establishment of a United Nations Emergency Force (UNEF. Within a matter of weeks Hammarskjöld was able to establish the force and arrange for its operation along the lines between Israel and Egypt.

In 1958 Hammarskjöld was reelected as secretary general. He increasingly turned his attention to the emerging nations of Asia and Africa.

In July 1960 he became involved in attempting to solve the civil war in the Congo. He arranged for a UN peace-keeping force to be sent to the region but in September 1961 fighting erupted between Katanga troops and the non-combatant forces of the UN. In an effort to secure a cease-fire he arranged to meet President Moise Tshombe. En route, on September 17 Hammarskjöld and 15 others were killed when their plane crashed in Northern Rhodesia (Zambia).

Hammarskjöld was awarded the Nobel Prize for peace posthumously in 1961. His journal, *Markings,* was published in 1963.

❖❖❖

50
Audrey Hepburn
(1929-1993)

Audrey Hepburn was a Belgian-born, Dutch-raised actress and philanthropist of British and Dutch ancestry. With Roman Holiday (1953) she won an Oscar. From 1988 on she worked for UNICEF.

Audrey Hepburn was born on May 4, 1929 in Brussels, Belgium.

Audrey went to London with her mother where she went to a private girls' school. Later, when her mother moved back to the Netherlands, she attended private schools as well.

Audrey went to a ballet school in London on a scholarship and later began a modelling career.

After being spotted modeling by a producer, she was signed to a bit part in the European film Nederlands in 7 lessen (1948) in 1948. Later, she had a speaking role in the 1951 film, *Young Wives' Tale* (1951) as Eve Lester.

Audrey gained immediate prominence in the US with her role in *Roman Holiday* (1953) in 1953. This

film turned out to be a smashing success as she won an Oscar as Best Actress. This gained her enormous popularity and more plum roles.

Roman Holiday (1953) was followed by another similarly wonderful performance in the 1957 classic *Funny Face* (1957), *Sabrina (*1954), for which she received another Academy nomination, and *Love in the Afternoon* (1957). In 1959, she received yet another nomination for her role in *The Nun's Story* (1959). She reached the pinnacle of her career when she played Holly Golightly in the delightful film *Breakfast at Tiffany's* (1961. For this she received another nomination.

She scored commercial success again in the espionage caper *Charade* (1963). One of her most radiant roles was in the fine production of *My Fair Lady* (1964) in 1964. After a couple of other movies, most notably *Two for the Road* (1967), she hit pay dirt and another nomination in 1967's *Wait Until Dark* (1967). One film of note was *Robin and Marian* (1976), with Sean Connery in 1976.

In 1988, Audrey became a special ambassador to the United Nations UNICEF fund helping children in Latin America and Africa, a position she retained until 1993.

She was named to *People*'s magazine as one of the 50 most beautiful people in the world. Her last film was *Always* (1989).

Audrey Hepburn died on January 20, 1993 in Tolochnaz, Switzerland, from colon cancer.

❖❖❖

51

Edmund Percival Hillary

(1919-2007)

Edmund Hillary was was a New Zealand mountaineer and explorer. Hillary and his Sherpa guide Tenzing Norgay were the first humans to reach Earth's highest point: the summit of Mount Everest in the Himalayas on 29 May 1953. Hillary was promptly knighted for his feat and in later years led expeditions to the South Pole and to the source of the Yangtze River.

Edmund Hillary was born in Auckland, New Zealand, on July 20, 1919.

He spent his childhood in Tuakau, Auckland, where he went to the local primary school. Later he travelled daily to the city for secondary schooling.

In 1935, during a ski weekend on a school trip to Mount Ruapehu, Hillary discovered his joy in the mountains and it never left him. He would often escape to the mountains to enjoy skiing and hiking, and he developed a love of climbing. A few years later he climbed his first mountain, the 7,500-foot Mount Oliver in New Zealand.

Hillary enlisted with the Royal New Zealand Air Force in World War II. While serving as a navigator in the South Pacific, he was wounded in battle. Despite the physical setback, Hillary was determined to make a full recovery and resume mountain climbing During the 1940s, Hillary made many climbs in New Zealand, particularly in the Southern Alps. Then came climbs in Europe that brought the invitation to join Sir John Hunt's expedition to Mount Everest, in the Himalaya Mountains in Nepal.

For two years, Hillary joined Hunt in the Scottish Highlands and in March 1953, along with twenty other of the best climbers in the world, they gathered at Everest. With the party's base camp just 1,100 feet from the summit, Hunt sent a two-man team the rest of the way. They failed but returned to camp with valuable information about how to attack the summit. Next, Hunt chose Hillary and Sherpa guide Tenzing Norgay (1914–1986) to make an attempt. After a heroic and death-defying climb, the two reached the summit on May 29, 1953, becoming the first two people to reach the top of the world. The successful climb in 1953 was jointly sponsored by the Royal Geographic Society and the Joint Himalayan Committee of the Alpine Club.

After the Everest expedition, Hillary gained worldwide fame and a reputation as an adventurer. Vivian Fuchsasked Hillary to become part of the Trans-Antarctic expedition in 1957 and 1958 that would cross the southern Atlantic Ocean to the South Pole. Hillary's job was to set up supply dumps from base camp towards the South Pole so that Fuchs's party could complete the crossing of Antarctica. Hillary wanted to use the sophisticated Snow-Cats available to Fuchs, but he had to settle for Ferguson farm tractors for transport and hauling. When the last dump was established, Hillary made his own decision to head for the Pole, which he reached with his three tractors on January 4, 1958. He was the first person to travel there by land in forty-six years.

Through the 1960s and 1970s, Hillary continued to explore the Himalayas. He also led a renowned expedition by jet boat and on foot from the mouth of the Ganges River to its source.

Hillary built hospitals and schools in the mountains of Nepal. He was president of Volunteer Service Abroad and patron of an Outdoor Pursuit Centre and of the Race Relations Council. He was also active in the Family Planning Association and in conservation campaigns.

Hillary was knighted in 1953. In 1985 he was appointed New Zealand High Commissioner to India. He was also honorary President for New York's Explorers Club.

His books include the Everest memoir *High Adventure* (1955) and his autobiography *Nothing Venture, Nothing Win* (1975).

He died at home in New Zealand at the age of 88 in 2007.

❖❖❖

52
Alfred Joseph Hitchcock
(1899-1980)

Sir Alfred Joseph Hitchcock was a British filmmaker and producer who pioneered many techniques in the suspense and psychological thriller genres. He received the American Film Institute's lifetime achievement award and was knighted in England.

Alfred Joseph Hitchcock was born in London on August 13, 1899.

Alfred was educated at St. Ignatius College, but left school at 16 to study engineering and navigation at the University of London. Three years later, he started work as an estimator at Henley Telegraph Company. Hitchcock moved into the advertising department shortly after.

Hitchcock's keen interest in cinema and art happily coincided with a job opening at Paramount studios in London as a title designer for silent films. He worked his way up to assistant director and in 1922, at the age of 22, started work on the film *Number Thirteen.*

By 1923, he was a scenario writer for Gainsborough Pictures in Islington, England, and that same year he saw his first credit as art director for *Woman to Woman*. He later became co-director of the film *Always Tell Your Wife*. He then acted as designer, script collaborator, and assistant director on *The White Shadow* (1923) and *The Passionate Adventure* (1924). *The Prude's Fall* (1924) and *The Blackguard* (1925) both followed.

With *The Pleasure Garden* (1925), Hitchcock debuted as a director. He returned to the German studio Emelka for his second film, *The Mountain Eagle* (1926), which was also shot on location in the Austrian Tyrol. His next film, *The Lodger* (1926), was a success and launched his career in England. He soon became the most successful and highest-paid director in England. Somehow his next film didn't measure up to his previous success. It was appropriately, and ironically, called *Downhill* (1927. An early example of Hitchcock's technical virtuosity was his creation of "subjective sound" for *Blackmail* (1929), his first sound film.

In *Murder* (1930), Hitchcock first made explicit the link between sex and violence. *The Man Who Knew Too Much* (1934), a commercial and critical success, established a favorite pattern: an investigation of family relationships within a suspenseful story. *The 39 Steps* (1935) showcases a mature Hitchcock; it is a stylish and efficiently told chase film brimming with exciting incidents and memorable characters. Despite their merits, both *The Secret Agent* and *Sabotage* (both 1936) exhibited flaws Hitchcock later acknowledged and learned from. *The Lady Vanishes* (1938), on the other hand, is sleek, exemplary Hitchcock: fast-paced, witty, and magnificently entertaining.

Hitchcock emigrated to the U.S. to direct *Rebecca* (1940). While the film won an Oscar, Hitchcock did not win for Best Director. Hitchcock's last British film, *Jamaica Inn* (1939), and his first Hollywood effort, *Rebecca* (1940), were both handsomely mounted though somewhat uncharacteristic works based on novels by Daphne du Maurier. Despite its somewhat muddled narrative, *Foreign Correspondent* (1940) was the first Hollywood film in his recognizable style. *Suspicion* (1941) was an exploration of family dynamics; its introduction of evil into the domestic arena foreshadowed *Shadow of a Doubt* (1943).

Some of his psychological dramas of the late 1940s were *Shadow, Lifeboat* (1944), *Spellbound* (1945), *Notorious* (1946), *The Paradine Case* (1947), *Rope* (1948), *Under Capricorn* (1949) and *Strangers on a Train* (1951).

The decade 1950-1960 was an amazingly productive one for Hitchcock. He produced a cycle of memorable films which included *I Confess* (1953), *Dial M for Murder* (1954), *To Catch a Thief* (1955),

The Man Who Knew Too Much (1956), *The Trouble with Harry* (1955). He also directed several top-drawer films like *Strangers on a Train* and *The Wrong Man* (1956), four masterpieces: *Rear Window, Vertigo, North by Northwest,* and *Psycho.*

In 1955 Hitchcock became a U.S. citizen and launched *Alfred Hitchcock Presents,* the TV show that catapulted him from lauded director and celebrity to icon. He wrote, produced and directed films up until 1979. His best-known later works include *The Birds, Marnie, Torn Curtain, Topaz, Frenzy* and *Family Plot.*

He died in 1980 in Los Angeles.

❖❖❖

53

Dorothy Crowfoot Hodgkin

(1910–1994)

Dorothy Hodgkin was a British chemist, credited with the discovery of protein crystallography.She pioneered the technique of X-ray crystallography, a method used to determine the three dimensional structures of biomolecules. For her work with vitamin B-12, she was awarded the Nobel Prize in chemistry in 1964.

Dorothy Crowfoot Hodgkin was born in Egypt on May 12, 1910.

In 1921, she entered the Leman School. Her excellent early education prepared her well for university. She was later educated at Somerville College, Oxford.

She also studied in Cambridge under the tutelage of John Desmond Bernal where she became aware of the potential of X-ray crystallography to determine the structure of proteins. After a brief period as a postgraduate student at Cambridge University, she returned to Oxford in 1934 and spent her entire academic career there.

In 1936, she became a research fellow at Somerville College, Oxford, a post which she held until 1977. In 1960 she was appointed Wolfson Research Professor at the Royal Society

Dorothy determined the three-dimensional structures of the following biomolecules: cholesterol in 1937, penicillin in 1945, vitamin B12 in 1954, insulin in 1969 as well as lactoglobulin, ferritin, and tobacco mosaic virus. The list is not exhaustive, it rather highlights major milestones.

Insulin was one of Dorothy Hodgkin's extraordinary quests. It began in 1934 when she was offered a small sample of crystalline insulin by Robert Robinson. The hormone captured her imagination because of the intricate and wide-ranging effect it has in the body. However, at this stage X-ray crystallography had not been developed far enough to cope with the complexity of the insulin molecule. She and others spent many years improving the technique. Larger and more complex molecules were being tackled until in 1969, the structure of insulin was finally resolved. But her quest was not finished then. She cooperated with other laboratories active in insulin research, gave advice, and travelled the world giving talks about insulin and it importance for diabetes. She considered solving the structure of insulin her greatest scientific achievement.

She received many honours but was more interested in exchange with other scientists. She was President of Pugwash from 1976 to 1988. In 1964 she was awarded the Nobel Prize in Chemistry for her work in crystallography and in 1976 the Copley Medal from the Royal Society. In 1965 she was appointed to the Order of Merit, filling the vacancy left by Winston Churchill.

Hodgkin died of a stroke on July 29, 1994, in Shipston-on-Stour, England.

❖❖❖

54

Maqbool Fida Hussain

(1915-)

Maqbool Fida Hussain is a world famous painter and an icon among Indian artists In 1966, the Government of India awarded him the prestigious Padma Shree. He has also been awarded the Padma Bhushan. The Government of India also appointed him to a term in the Rajya Sabha, in recognition of his contribution to art.

MF Hussain was born on September 17, 1915 in Pandharpur, Maharashtra.

Hussain did his schooling from Indore. In 1935, he moved to Bombay and joined Sir J. J. School of Art. He started off by painting cinema hoardings. He first came into limelight as painter in the late 1940s.

In the 1947 annual exhibition of the Bombay Art Society, his painting *Sunhera Sansaar* was shown. This was his first exhibition.

In 1947, he joined the Progressive Artists' Group, founded by Francis Newton Souza. This was a clique of young artists who wished to break with the nationalist traditions established by the Bengal school of art and to encourage an Indian avant-garde, engaged at an international level. Through it, Husain was exposed to, and strongly influenced by, the work of Emil Nolde and Oskar Kokoschka. From 1948 to 1950 a series of exhibitions all over India brought Husain's work to the notice of the public.

In 1952, his first solo exhibition was held at Zürich and over the next few years, his work was widely seen in Europe and U.S.

In 1955, he was awarded the prestigious Padma Shree prize by the Government of India.

In the following year he made his first film, *Through the Eyes of a Painter*. It was shown at the Berlin Festival and won a Golden Bear.

Some of his best known works are called the Sufi paintings, and were first exhibited at the Pundole Gallery in 1978.

During the 1980s Hussain slowly grew into a public figure, often embroiled in controversies. Many a time he has been charged with hurting sentiments of people because of his nude portraits of Hindu gods and goddesses His *Shwetambari* exhibition at the Jehangir Art Gallery consisted of two halls shrouded in white cloth, whorls of which also shared the floor with torn newspapers. Later, he gave a public performance at the Tata Centre in Calcutta. For several days a crowd watched as he painted pictures of six goddesses. On the last day of the exhibition he destroyed his paintings by overpainting with white.

He was nominated to the upper house of the Indian Parliament, the Rajya Sabha in 1987; and during his six year term he produced the Sansad Portfolio.

In the early 1990s, several collections of his paintings were made accessible to the public in exhibitions of permanent galleries. The most interesting of these is the *Hussain-Doshi Gufa* in Ahmadabad, a collaboration between the painter and an architect in the construction of a gallery. His most interesting paintings of this period are the series named after the film-star Madhuri Dixit.

Hussain started directing and producing movies also. His movies include *Gaja Gamini* (with Madhuri Dixit) and *Meenaxi: A Tale of Three Cities* (with Tabu). The autobiography of M.F. Hussain is being made into a movie, which has been tentatively titled as *The Making of the Painter.* So huge is the popularity of his paintings that he was once called as the 'Picasso of India' by the *Forbes magazine.*

❖❖❖

55

Joan of Arc

(1412-1431)

Saint Joan of Arc, also known as the Maid of Orleans, is a national heroine of France and a Catholic saint. She led the French army to several important victories during the Hundred Years' War, claiming divine guidance, and was indirectly responsible for the coronation of Charles VII. She was beatified in 1909 and later canonised in 1920.

Joan of Arc, or Jehanne la Pucelle, as she was known in her day, was born on January 6, 1412, in Domremy, Champagne, France.

She was an unusually pious child, frequently went to church and immersed herself in prayer. It was around the age of 13, that she received the first of her visions. She described a blaze of light accompanying it, and she identified it as St. Michael. Michael told her that she would be visited soon by Sts. Catherine and Margaret. When St. Margaret and St. Catherine appeared, they soon revealed her mission to her, that she must help deliver the French people from the English, win back Orleans, and see the dauphin Charles VII crowned king at Rheims.

She left Domremy and rode to the nearby city of Vaucouleurs, with her uncle. There, she was to convince the town's captain, Sir Robert de Baudricourt, of her mission and request an escort to Chinon. At their first meeting, in 1428, he was stubborn and refused to believe her. The next month, he reluctantly agreed to send her there after she described a French defeat as it happened, a battle known as the "Day of the Herrings". A courier confirmed her report a few days later.

Then, she was assigned an escort of six men. She arrived at Chinon on 4 March. Two days later, she had the audience with Charles. But Charles was already not convinced of her divine mission. So, he decided to test her by disguising himself as a courtier. She picked out Charles from the crowd and presented herself to him. She convinced him of her mission and showed him signs from God, ones which he was not to reveal to anyone.

A banner and a suit of armour were also made for her. She was given the St. Catherine's Sword, with five crosses embossed on the blade near the hilt. It was the sword used by the grandfather of Charlemagne, Charles Martel, during his defence of France from the Muslims in 732. Then she rode off to free Orleans. She audaciously summoned the English to remove their troops from French soil. The English were infuriated with her boldness. She entered Orleans on April 29.

On May 2, Joan launched an attack to regain the bastides from the English. On May 4, the Saint-Loup bastide was taken. By May 7, the remaining bastides were taken by the French. That day, Joan was wounded in the breast by an arrow. But she returned to fight. She proceeded with haste, because her counsel had told her she had little more than a year left in the army. She was wounded again in the campaign, but again, she miraculously recovered.

John, the Duke d'Alencon, joined Joan at Jargeau on June 11. The city was taken in two days. The attacks on Meung-sur-Loire, Beaugency, and Patay, each lasted one day. Patay was by far the greatest victory of Joan's career. The French totally massacred the English. With much pomp and celebration, the dauphin Charles was crowned King at Rheims Cathedral on July 17, 1429.

Thus ended Joan's mission, and her voices began to go silent. She wanted to return home to Domremy and be with her family again. Yet, Charles held her against her will. She led an attack with Charles on Paris in early September. Though St-Denis was occupied by the French without opposition, the attack failed, and Joan herself was wounded again, with a crossbolt through the thigh. The Duke d'Alencon removed her almost by force, and the attack was abandoned. The retreat harmed Joan's prestige, and she sadly laid down her arms at the altar in St-Denis.

She returned to the field in April, and her voices had told her she was to be captured before the Midsummer Day. She had come to the aid of Compiegne on May 24, 1430, to defend them from the Burgundian attack. By some mistake or panic of Guillaume de Flavy, the drawbridge to Compiegne was raised during a Burgundian attack, and Joan was not able to get back inside. A Burgundian archer snatched her from her horse, and she was taken off, kicking and screaming. After a few months and a couple escape attempts, Joan was removed from Beaurevoir fortress, and was sold to the English, who closely guarded their prisoner. The English would soon try her for heresy.

Her examination ended on March 17. She was sentenced to be burned at the stake, and it was to be carried out two days later. As she was led to the stake, she cried out for someone to give her a cross. An English soldier quickly made one and gave it to her, and she promptly put it under her garments. When the flames were lit, she called out continuously on the Holy Name of Jesus, until she breathed her last. In spite of numerous attempts by the executioner to finish the job, her heart remained intact and full of blood, along with her other entrails. The executioner was astonished at this as if it were a confirmed miracle.

As Joan had predicted, by 1453, the French and Burgundians had driven the English off of French soil.

In April 1909, Joan was beatified. On May 16, 1920, she was canonised a saint at St. Peter's Basilica in Rome by Pope Benedict

XV. It was decided that her feast day would be May 30, the day of her execution at the stake, 489 years before. She is the patron saint of France and also of all who must take up arms in defence of their country.

❖❖❖

56

Carl Gustav Jung

(1875–1961)

Carl Gustav Jung was a Swiss psychiatrist, an influential thinker and the founder of analytical psychology. In 1948 he founded the C. G. Jung Institute in Zurich.

Carl Jung was born on July 26, 1875, in Kesswil, Switzerland.

When he was six years old, he went to the village school in Klein-Huningen. His father also started teaching him Latin at this time.

He studied medicine at the University of Basel (1895–1900). He received his medical degree from the University of Zurich in 1902. Later he studied psychology in Paris, France.

Jung began his professional career in 1900 as an assistant to Eugen Bleuler at the psychiatric clinic of the University of Zurich. Jung, with a few associates, worked out the so-called association experiment — a method of testing used to reveal affectively significant groups of ideas in the unconscious area of the psyche (the mind). These groups or "complexes" would have a control over the affected person, and would encourage anxieties and inappropriate emotions.

When Jung read Sigmund Freud's *Interpretation of Dreams,* he found his own ideas and observations to be basically confirmed and furthered. He sent his publication *Studies in Word Association* (1904) to Freud, and this was the beginning of their Notable Biographies.

Jung was eager to explore the secrets of the unconscious psyche expressed by dreaming, fantasies, myths, fairy tales, superstition and occultism. For him the unconscious not only is a disturbing factor causing psychic illnesses but also is basically the source of man's creativeness and the roots of a person's consciousness. With such ideas Jung came increasingly into conflict with Freud, who regarded Jung's ideas as unscientific.

During the years from 1913 to 1921 Jung published only three important papers: "Two Essays on Analytical Psychology" (1916, 1917) and "Psychological Types" (1921). The former provided the basic ideas from which his later work was developed. He described his research on psychological typology. He expressed the idea that it is the "personal equation" which influences how an individual observes and interacts with their world.

Next to Jung's typology, his main contribution was his discovery that man's fantasy life has a certain structure. There must be subtle active centres in the unconscious which control natural behaviouur and free imagination. These combine to form Jung's concept of archetypes. An individual will dream on impulse, and these dreams will have a theme or story similar to a fairy tale, or a myth, from a time long past, that are unknown to the person dreaming. To Jung this meant that archetypal symptoms belong to human beings of all ages and from all times; they are the expression of a collective body of man's basic psychic nature.

In order to study archetypal patterns and processes, Jung visited so-called primitive tribes. He lived among the Pueblo Indians of New Mexico and Arizona in 1924 and 1925 and among the inhabitants of Mt. Elgon in Kenya during 1925 and 1926. He later visited Egypt and India. To Jung, the religious symbols and phenomenology of Buddhism and Hinduism and the teachings of Zen Buddhism and Confucianism all expressed differentiated experiences on the way to man's inner world, a world which was badly neglected by Western civilisation.

Jung also searched for traditions in Western culture, which made up for its one-sided outgoing development toward reason and technology. He found these traditions in Gnosticism, Christian mysticism and occultism.

His career included the professorship of medical psychology at the University of Basel and the titular professorship of philosophy from 1933 until 1942 on the faculty of philosophical and political sciences of the Federal Institute of Technology in Zurich.

His most famous books include *Psychology and Religion* (1937), *The Undiscovered Self* (1957) and his autobiography, *Memories, Dreams, Reflections* (1962).

In 1948 he founded the C.G. Jung Institute in Zurich. Honorary doctorates were conferred on him by many important universities all over the world

Carl Gustav Jung died in Küsnacht on June 6, 1961.

❖❖❖

57

Kalidasa

(c. A.D.400-?)

Kalidasa is one of the greatest Sanskrit poets that India has ever had. The poems he wrote were usually of epic proportions and were written in classical Sanskrit. His place in Sanskrit literature is akin to that of Shakespeare in English. His plays and poetry are primarily based on Hindu mythology and philosophy.

An Indian poet and dramatist, Kalidasa lived sometime between the reign of Agnimitra, the second Shunga king (c.170 B.C.) who was the hero of one of his dramas, and the Aihole inscription of A.D. 634 which praises Kalidasa's poetic skills. Most scholars now associate him with the reign of Chandragupta II (reigned c. 380-c. 415).

Virtually no facts are known about his life, although colourful legends abound. He became the most brilliant of the 'nine gems' at the court of Vikramaditya of Ujjain.

Kalidasa was well acquainted with contemporary sciences and arts, including politics and astronomy. His knowledge of scientific astronomy was manifestly gleaned from Greek sources.

Kalidasa's first surviving play, *Malavikagnimitra* or *Malavika and Agnimitra*, tells the story of the love of Agnimitra of Vidisha, king of the Shungas, for the beautiful handmaiden of his chief queen. In the end she is discovered to be of royal birth and is accepted as one of his queens. The play contains an account of the raajasuuya sacrifice performed by Pushyamitra, and a rather tiresome exposition of a theory on music and acting. It is not a play of the first order.

Kalidasa's second play, generally considered his masterpiece, is the *Shakuntala*. A theme borrowed from the *Mahabharata*, it is a drama in seven acts, a masterpiece of dramatic skill and poetic diction, expressing tender and passionate sentiments with gentleness and moderation, so lacking in most Indian literary works. It received enthusiastic praise from Goethe.

The last of Kalidasa's surviving plays, *Vikramorvashe* or *Urvashi Conquered by Valour*, is more mystical than the earlier plays. It is a drama of the trotaka class relating how king Pururavas rescues the nymph Urvashii from the demons. Summoned by Indra he is obliged to part from her. The fourth act on the madness of Pururavas is unique. Apart from the extraordinary soliloquy of the demented lover in search of his beloved, it contains several verses in Prakrit.

In *Meghaduuta* (Cloud Messenger), the theme of this long lyrical poem is a message sent by an exiled yaksha in Central India to his wife in the Himalayas, his envoy being a *megha* or cloud. Its beautiful descriptions of nature and the delicate expressions of love in which passion is purified and desire ennobled, likewise won the admiration of Goethe.

Raghuvamsha (Raghu's genealogy), a *mahakavya*, regarded as Kalidasa's best work, describes the life of Rama with a record of his ancestors and descendants.

Ritu-samhaara (Seasonal Cycle) is a poem describing the six seasons of the year in all their changing aspects.

Kumara-sambhava (Kumara's Occasioning), usually

translated 'The Birth of the War-god', is a *mahakavya* relating how Parvati won the love of Shiva in order to bring into the world Kumara (i.e. Karttikeya), the god of war, to destroy the demon Taraka.

❖❖❖

58

Har Gobind Khorana

(1922-)

Dr. Har Gobind Khorana is recipient of the Nobel Prize for Medicine and Physiology along with Marshall Nirenberg and Robert Holley for cracking the genetic code.

Dr. Har Gobind Khorana was born on 9 January 1922 at Raipur, Punjab (now in Pakistan).

He obtained his M.Sc. Honours in Organic Chemistry from the Punjab University in 1945 and later received his Ph. D. from the University of Liverpool in England.

Dr. Khorana spent a year in Zurich in 1948-49 as a post-doctoral fellow at the Swiss Federal Institute of Technology and returned to India for a brief period in 1949.

He returned to England in 1950 and spent two years on a fellowship at Cambridge and began research on nucleic acids under Sir Alexander Todd and Kenner. His interest in proteins and nucleic acids took root at that time.

In 1952 he went to the University of British Columbia, Vancouver on a job offer and there a group began to work in the field of biologically interesting phosphate esters and nucleic acids with the inspiration from Dr. Gordon M. Shrum and Scientific counsel from Dr. Jack Campbell.

In 1960 he joined the University of Wisconsin as Professor and Co-Director of the Institute of Enzyme Research and Professor of Biochemistry (1962-70) and became an US citizen.

He continued research on nucleic acid synthesis and prepared the first artificial copy of a yeast gene. He is also the first to synthesize oligonucleotides, that is, strings of nucleotides. These custom designed pieces of artificial genes are widely used in biology labs for sequencing, cloning and engineering new plants and animals. The oligo nucleotides, thus, have become indispensable tools in biotechnology.

In 1970 he became the Alfred Sloan Professor of Biology and Chemistry at the Massachusetts Institute of Technology, Cambridge, USA. He was elected a member of the National Academy of Sciences, Washington as well as a Fellow of the American Association for the Advancement of Science.

In 1971 he became a foreign member of USSR Academy of Sciences and in 1974 Honorary Fellow of the Indian Chemical Society.

He won the Nobel Prize for Medicine in 1968 sharing it with M.W. Nuremberg and R.W. Holley for interpreting the genetic code and analysing its function in protein synthesis. The other awards conferred on him include Distinguished Service Awards. Watumull Foundation, Honolulu, Hawaii (1968); American Academy of Achievement Award, Philadelphia, Pennsylvania (1971); Padma Vibhushan, Presidential Award, India (1972); J.C.Bose Medal, Bose Institute, Calcutta (1972) and Willard Gibbs medal of the Chicago Section of American Chemical Society (1973-74).

He continues to work as an Emeritus and Senior Lecturer at University of Liverpool.

❖❖❖

59

Martin Luther King

(1929-1968)

Martin Luther King, Jr. was an American Baptist minister and social activist who led the civil rights movement in the United States from the mid-1950s until his death by assassination in 1968. He was awarded the Nobel Prize for Peace in 1964.

Martin Luther King, Jr. was born on January 15, 1929 in Atlanta, Georgia.

He began his education at the Yonge Street Elementary School in Atlanta, Georgia, then enrolled in David T. Howard Elementary School. He also attended the Atlanta University Laboratory School and Booker T. Washington High School.

In 1948, he graduated from Morehouse College with a B.A. degree in Sociology. That fall, he enrolled in Crozer Theological Seminary in Chester, Pennsylvania. While attending Crozer, he also studied at the University of Pennsylvania. He was elected president of the senior class and delivered the valedictory address; he won the Pearl Plafker Award for the most outstanding student; and he received the J. Lewis Crozer fellowship for graduate study at a university of his choice. He was awarded a Bachelor of Divinity degree from Crozer in 1951.

The Ph.D. degree from Boston, a Doctorate of Philosophy in Systematic Theology, was awarded to him on June 5, 1955.

He was the pastor of Dexter Avenue from September 1954 to November 1959, when he resigned to move to Atlanta to direct the activities of the Southern Christian Leadership Conference. From 1960 until his death in 1968, he was co-pastor with his father at Ebenezer Baptist Church and President of the Southern Christian Leadership Conference.

Dr. King was a pivotal figure in the Civil Rights Movement. He was elected president of the Montgomery Improvement Association, the organisation which was responsible for the successful Montgomery Bus Boycott from 1955 to 1956 (381 days). He was arrested thirty times for his participation in civil rights activities.

He was a founder and president of Southern Christian Leadership Conference from 1957 to 1968. He was also vice president of the national Sunday School and Baptist Teaching Union Congress of the National Baptist Convention. He was elected to membership in several learned societies including the prestigious American Academy of Arts and Sciences.

Dr. King received several hundred awards for his leadership in the Civil Rights Movement. In 1964, at age 35, Dr. King was the youngest man, the second American, and the third black man to be awarded the Nobel Peace Prize.

His lectures and remarks stirred the concern and sparked the conscience of a generation; the movements and marches he led brought significant changes in the fabric of American life; his courageous and selfless devotion gave direction to thirteen years of civil rights activities; his charismatic leadership inspired men and women, young and old, in the nation and abroad.

Dr. King's speech at the march on Washington in 1963, his acceptance speech of the Nobel Peace Prize, his last sermon at Ebenezer Baptist Church, and his final speech in Memphis are among his most famous utterances (I've Been to the Mountaintop). The Letter from Birmingham Jail ranks among the most important American documents. King wrote *Stride toward Freedom* (1958), *Why We Can't Wait* (1964), and *Where Do We Go from Here: Chaos or Community?* (1967).

Dr. King was shot while standing on the balcony of the Lorraine Motel in Memphis, Tennessee on April 4, 1968, by James Earl Ray.

The Martin Luther King, Jr. Historic Site, a 23 acre area was listed as a National Historic Landmark on May 5, 1977, and was made a National Historic Site on October 10, 1980 by the U.S. Department of the Interior. His birthday is a national holiday, celebrated on the third Monday in January.

❖❖❖

60

Verghese Kurien

(1921-)

Verghese Kurien is called the father of the White Revolution in India. He is also known as the Milkman of India. He was the architect behind the success of the largest dairy development programme in the world, christened as Operation Flood. He was awarded the 1963 Ramon Magsaysay Award for Community Leadership. He was also awarded with Padma Shri (1965), Padma Bhushan (1966), and Padma Vibhushan (1999).

Verghese Kurien was born on November 26, 1921 in Kozhikode, Kerala.

Kurien graduated with Physics from Loyola College, Madras in 1940. Subsequently, he did his B.E.(Mechanical) from the Madras University and went to USA on a government scholarship to do his Masters in Mechanical Engineering from Michigan State University. In between, he completed special studies in engineering at the Tata Iron and Steel Company Institute at Jamshedpur, Bihar, in February 1946 and underwent nine months of specialised training in dairy engineering at the National Dairy Research Institute of Bangalore

Dr. Verghese Kurien returned from America in 1948 and joined the Dairy Department of the Government of India. In May 1949, he was posted as Dairy Engineer at the Government Research Creamery in Anand, Gujarat. Around this time, the newly formed cooperative dairy, Kaira District Cooperative Milk Producers' Union Limited ((KDCMPUL), was engaged in a battle of survival with the privately owned Polson Dairy, which was a giant in its field. Enthused by the challenge, Kurien left his government job and volunteered to help Shri Tribhuvandas Patel, the Chairman of KDCMPUL, to set up a processing plant. This led to the birth of AMUL.

In 1965, Prime Minister Lal Bahadur Shastri created the National Dairy Development Board under the leadership of Kurien to replicate the success story of Amul throughout the country.

In 1973, Kurien set up the Gujarat Cooperative Milk Marketing Federation to market the products of the dairies. Under his stewardship India became the largest producer of milk in the world.

During his illustrious career, Kurien won many accolades and awards: Ramon Magsaysay Award for Community Leadership (1963), Padma Shri (1965), Padma Bhushan (1966), Krishi Ratna Award (1986), Wateler Peace Prize Award of Carnegie Foundation (1986), World Food Prize Laureate (1989), International Person of the Year (1993) by the World Dairy Expo, Madison, Wisconsin, USA, and Padma Vibhushan (1999).

Dr. Kurien still remains an active member of the international community, holding positions ranging from the Chancellor of the University of Allahabad since April of 2006 to a member of the Advisory Committee of the South Asian Network on Fermented Foods, and chairman of the Viksit Bharat Foundation.

61

Rani Lakshmibai

(1828-1858)

Lakshmibai, (The Rani of Jhansi), the queen of the Maratha-ruled princely state of Jhansi in North India, was one of the leading figures of the Indian Rebellion of 1857, and a symbol of resistance to British rule in India. Remembered as the "Joan of India', she remains a major figure in the pantheon of Indian nationalist icon.

Rani Lakshmibai was born on 19 November 1828 at Varanasi. She was named Manikarnikka at birth.

She completed her studies and learned horse riding, shooting, elephant riding and much more. She not only trained men for a historic war but also included the Indian women.

Lakshmibai gave birth to a son in 1851, but unfortunately this child died when he was about four months old. After this tragedy, the couple adopted a son. To ensure that the British did not raise an issue over the adoption, Lakshmibai got this adoption witnessed by the local British representatives. After the death of her husband, Maharaja Gangadhar Rao, she was eighteen years old. She did not lose her courage. She always remembered her responsibility.

At that time Lord Dalhousie was the Governor-General of India. The adopted child was named Damodar Rao. As per the Hindu tradition, he was their legal heir. However, the British rulers refused to accept him as the legal heir. As per the Doctrine of Lapse, Lord Dalhousie decided to seize the state of Jhansi. Lakshmibai consulted a British lawyer. Thereafter, she filed an appeal for the hearing of her case in London. But, her plea was rejected. The British authorities confiscated the state jewels. Also, an order was passed asking the Rani to leave Jhansi fort and move to the Rani Mahal in Jhansi. Laxmibai was firm about protecting the state of Jhansi.

Jhansi became the focal point of an uprising. She began to strengthen her position. By seeking the support of others, she formed a volunteer army, consisting of not only menfolk, but also women. Women were also given military training to fight a battle. In the revolt, Lakshmibai was accompanied by her generals.

From the period September-October 1857, Rani defended Jhansi from being invaded by the armies of the neighbouring rajas of Orchha and Datia. In January 1858, the British army headed its away towards Jhansi. The conflict went on for two weeks. Finally, the British succeeded in the annexation of the city. However, Lakshmibai managed to escape along with her son, strapped tightly to her back, in the guise of a man She took refuge in Kalpi, where she met Tatya Tope, a great warrior. Again a fierce battle took place. Rani Jhansi fought with deathless patriotism and martyrdom. However on the second day of the fighting, the great heroine of the first struggle for India freedom, at the age of 22 years, lost her life.

The black day was June 17, 1858. It is believed that, when she was lying unconscious in the battlefield, a Brahmin found her and brought her to an ashram, where she died.

For her immense effort, she is referred to as the 'Icon of the Indian Nationalist Movement'. Throughout the uprising, the aim of Lakshmibai was to secure the throne for her adopted son Damodar. Her story became a beacon for the upcoming generations of freedom fighters.

❖❖❖

62

Rasipuram Krishnaswamy Laxman

(1924-)

R.K. Laxman is an Indian cartoonist, illustrator and humorist. He is widely regarded as India's greatest-ever cartoonist and is best known for his creation The Common Man. He has written and published numerous short stories, essays and travel articles. He was awarded the prestigious Padma Bhushan and Asia's top journalism award, the Ramon Magsaysay Award.

Rasipuram Krishnaswamy Iyer Laxman was born on 23 October 1924 in Mysore.

Laxman was admitted at a nearby municipal primary school. He had a passion for sketching since childhood. He used to draw street scenes, people and landscapes. One day he found three broken glass panes in red, blue and green, offering him a world of magic – turning the landscape into different colours; an entire garden, trees, flowers, the gardener etc. drenched in green. He used to gather his father's magazines and get lost looking at the large illustrations. His favourite magazine was *Strand.* He also read *Bystander, Wide World, Tit Bits* and *Punch.* He used to read jokes under the cartoons, which developed his visualisation and sense of humour.

While still at the Maharaja's College, Mysore, studying politics, economics and philosophy, he began to illustrate his elder brother R K Narayan's stories in *The Hindu.* He was behind the distinctive illustrations in the Malgudi stories written RK Narayan. He drew political cartoons for the local papers, and for the *Swatantra*. He held a summer job at the Gemini Studios, Madras.

After graduation Laxman went to Delhi to find a job as cartoonist. *The Hindustan Times* told him he was too young, that he should start with provincial papers. *The Free Press Journal* in Bombay had no such qualms. Laxman found himself seated next to another cartoonist who was furiously drawing a bird in a cage. His name was Bal Thackeray.

One day the Journal's proprietor banned him from making fun of communists. So the 23 year-old Laxman left, caught a Victoria, and walked into the *The Times of India* office. From that day, "I had a table and a room to myself which I have used ever since," he said. He feels oppressed by having to turn out a cartoon everyday. "Each morning I grumble, I plan to resign as I drag myself to the office. By the time I come home I like my work."

Laxman plays with every shade of humour — wit, satire, irony, slapstick, buffoonery, tragicomedy. Such versatility dazzles as does his unwearied discipline. No other cartoonist has understood the average Indian as Laxman has. This gives him a far wider reach than his sophisticated colleagues. From garbage disposal to nuclear physics, he can make you see every issue clearly and in a new light. His words have all the distinguishing features of a Laxman cartoon — the fine eye for detail, the pungent wit, the puckish sparkle, the sudden probe below the surface, and hearty guffaws at the absurdities of line.

Laxman's cartoons lay bare political hypocrisy and doublespeak with wit, insight and irony. His 'Common Man', who never speaks in the cartoons, manages to this day to raise important issues affecting the country, all with a generous dose of humour. His cartoon strip "You Said It", which features The Common Man, has attained cult status. He created the popular mascot for the Asian Paints Group called Gattu. Besides, he has written many books.

Besides the B.D. Goenka Award awarded by the Indian Express, the Ramon Magsaysay Award for Journalism, Literature and Creative

Communication Arts, he has awarded the Padma Bhushan and the Padma Vibhusan by the Union Government. Laxman was conferred the CNN-IBN Lifetime Achievement Award at the CNN-IBN Indian of the Year 2007.

❖❖❖

63

Vladimir Ilyich Lenin

(1870-1924)

Vladimir Ilyich Leninwas was a Russian revolutionary, a Bolshevik communist politician, the principal leader of the October Revolution and the first head of the Union of Soviet Socialist Republics. His contributions to Marxist theory are commonly referred to as Leninism.

Vladimir Ilich Lenin was born in Ulianovsk, Russia, on April 10, 1870.

Lenin was a bright student in school. He read the writings of Goethe and Turgenev that would affect him for life. He attended Kazan University where he studied law. Becoming interested in Marxism, he was involved in student protests and was subsequently expelled. He studied law on his own. It was during this period of exile that he first familiarised himself with Karl Marx's *Das Kapital.* He continued his studies at the University of Saint Petersburg, and, by 1891, had been admitted to the Bar. He also learnt Latin and Greek, German, French and English

Lenin practised as a lawyer for some years in Samara before moving to St Petersburg in 1893.

In 1895, he travelled to Switzerland to meet Social Democrats. When he returned to Russia, he planned to start a revolutionary paper, but he and the other leaders were arrested. He served 15 months in a prison, after which he was exiled to Siberia.

In 1900, his exile came to an end, and he began his travels throughout Russia and the rest of Europe. He lived in Zurich, Geneva, Munich, Prague, Vienna, Manchester and London, and, co-founded the newspaper *Iskra* (The Spark) with Julius Martov.

Lenin was active in the Russian Social Democratic Labour Party (RSDLP) and, soon rose to a position of power in the Social Democratic party. In 1906, Lenin was elected to the Presidium of the RSDLP but, almost from then right up until the revolutions of 1917, he spent the majority of his time exiled in Europe, where, despite a hard and bitter existence, he managed to continue his political writings. In response to philosophical debates on the proper course of a socialist revolution, Lenin completed *Materialism and Empirio-criticism* in 1909 a work which became fundamental in the Marxist-Leninist philosophy.

Lenin continued to travel in Europe and participated in many socialist meetings and activities, including the Prague Party Conference of 1912. When the First World War began in 1914, and the large Social Democratic parties of Europe supported their various countries' war efforts, Lenin was absolutely stunned, refusing to believe at first that the German Social Democrats had voted for war credits. This led him to a final split with the Second International, which was composed of these parties.

In 1914 Lenin moved to neutral Switzerland. In 1915 he attended the anti-war Zimmerwald Conference there. It was in Zurich in the spring of 1916 that he wrote the important theoretical work *Imperialism, the Highest Stage of Capitalism.* In this work Lenin argues that the merging of banks and industrial cartels give rise to finance capital.

In March 1917, steelworkers in St. Petersburg went on strike, with thousands of people lining the streets. The Tsar's power collapsed and the Duma, led by Alexander Kerensky, took power. Lenin fled to Finland for safety. Here he wrote his book *State and Revolution*, which called for a new form of government based on workers' councils, or soviets elected and revocable at all moments by the workers.

Lenin returned to Petrograd in October, inspiring the October Revolution with the slogan *All Power to the Soviets!* He directed the overthrow of the Provisional Government from the Smolny Institute from 6 to 8 November 1917. The storming and capitulation of the Winter Palace on these dates marked the beginning of Soviet rule.

Vladimir Lenin was named president of the Society of Peole's Commissars (Communist Party). Land was redistributed, some as collective farms. Factories, mines, banks and utilities were taken over by the state.

In May, 1922, Lenin suffered the first of a series of strokes. He died of a cerebral haemorrhage on January 21, 1924.

In 1998, he was named by *Time* magazine as one of the 100 most influential people of the 20th century.

❖❖❖

64
Leonardo da Vinci
(1452-1519)

Leonardo da Vinci was a Florentine artist, one of the great masters of the High Renaissance, a painter, sculptor, architect, engineer and scientist. His innovations in the field of painting influenced the course of Italian art for more than a century after his death, and his scientific studies—particularly in the fields of anatomy, optics, and hydraulics—anticipated many of the developments of modern science.

Leonardo was born on April 15, 1452, in the small Tuscan town of Vinci, near Florence.

He was given the best education that Florence, the intellectual and artistic centre of Italy, could offer. He rapidly advanced socially and intellectually. He was a fine musician and improviser.

In about 1466 he was apprenticed as a studio boy to Andrea del Verrocchio, the leading Florentine painter and sculptor of his day. In his workshop Leonardo was introduced to the painting of altarpieces and panel pictures to the creation of large sculptural projects in marble and bronze.

In 1478 Leonardo became an independent master. His first large painting, *The Adoration of the Magi,* left unfinished, was ordered in 1481 for the Monastery of San Donato a Scopeto, Florence. Other works are *Benois Madonna* (c. 1478, Hermitage, Saint Petersburg), the portrait *Ginerva de' Benci* (c.1474, National

Gallery, Washington, D.C.), and the unfinished *Saint Jerome* (c.1481, Pinacoteca, Vatican).

In about 1482 Leonardo entered the service of the duke of Milan, Ludovico Sforza. He served as principal engineer in the duke's numerous military enterprises and was active also as an architect. In addition, he assisted the Italian mathematician Luca Pacioli in the celebrated work *Divina Proportione* (1509). He spent 17 years in Milan. It was during these years that he hit his stride, reaching new heights of scientific and artistic achievement.

From 1485 to 1490, Leonardo produced studies on loads of subjects, including nature, flying machines, geometry, mechanics, municipal construction, canals and architecture (designing everything from churches to fortresses). His studies from this period contain designs for advanced weapons, including a tank and other war vehicles, various combat devices and submarines.

Alas, Leonardo's interests were so broad, and he was so often compelled by new subjects, that he usually failed to finish what he started. This resulted in his completing only about six works in these 17 years, including *The Last Supper* and *The Virgin on the Rocks*, and he left dozens of paintings and projects unfinished or unrealised.

Between 1490 and 1495 he developed his habit of recording his studies in meticulously illustrated notebooks. His work covered four main themes: painting, architecture, the elements of mechanics, and human anatomy. These studies and sketches were collected into various codices and manuscripts, which are now hungrily collected by museums and individuals.

Over the next 16 years, Leonardo designed a bridge to span the "golden horn" in Constantinople and received a commission, with the help of Machiavelli, to paint the *Battle of Anghiari*. He painted several portraits, but the only one that survives is the famous *Mona Lisa*, also known as *La Giocondaa* (1503-06, Louvre). It is as well known for its mastery of technical innovations as for the mysteriousness of its legendary smiling subject. This work is a consummate example of two techniques—sfumato and chiaroscuro—of which Leonardo was one of the first great masters.

From 1513 to 1516, he worked in Rome, maintaining a workshop and undertaking a variety of projects for the Pope. Following the death of his patron Giuliano de' Medici in March of 1516, he was offered the title of Premier Painter and Engineer and Architect of the King by Francis I in France. Although suffering from a paralysis of the right hand, he was still able to draw and teach. He produced studies for the Virgin Mary from *The Virgin and Child with St. Anne,* studies of cats, horses, dragons, St. George, anatomical studies, studies on the nature of water, drawings of the Deluge, and of various machines.

Leonardo died on May 2, 1519 in Cloux, France.

❖❖❖

65
Carl Lewis
(1961-)

Frederick Carlton Lewis is a retired American track and field athlete. In 1984 he became the first African American athlete since Jesse Owens (1913–1980) in 1936 to win four gold medals in Olympic competition. He won nine gold medals in four straight Olympics.

Frederick Carlton Lewis was born on July 1, 1961, in Birmingham, Alabama.

Lewis was not as talented as his brothers and sister. He kept working and practising the long jump in his back yard, determined to improve. He competed in track meets, and his dedication and confidence caught the eye of Jesse Owens himself at a meet in Philadelphia, Pennsylvania, calling him a "spunky little guy". When he graduated from Willingboro High School in 1979, Lewis was the top-ranked high school track athlete in the country.

In 1979 Lewis entered the University of Houston (Texas) on an athletic scholarship. Coach Tom Tellez suggested improvements in Lewis's style of jumping. After just one year of college Lewis qualified for the 1980 Olympic team, only to see opportunity pass him by when United States boycotted the Games in protest of the Soviet Union's invasion of Afghanistan. Lewis kept his top national ranking in the long jump and the 100-metre dash at the 1981 National Collegiate Athletic Association (NCAA) indoor championships, being the first athlete to win two events at an NCAA championship. He was awarded the Amateur Athletic Union's Sullivan Award.

In 1982 he worked at the Santa Monica Track Club in California. Coach Tellez continued to work closely with him. By 1983 he had become a winner in long jump, 100-metre run, 200-metre run, and 400-metre relay. He won three gold medals at the track and field world championships in Helsinki, Finland, in 1983. In 1984 he set an indoor world record in the long jump.

In Los Angeles, California, in the 1984 Summer Olympics he won the 100-metre sprint with a time of 9.99 seconds. His long jump effort of twenty-eight feet earned him a second gold. For his third, Lewis set an Olympic record with a 19.8-second run in the 200-metre race. Finally, he led the 400-metre relay team to an Olympic record victory at 37.83 seconds. He was mocked by writers as "King Carl" for his brash predictions and for showing up late to press conferences. An endorsement contract with Nike was cancelled, but in Europe and Japan he became a hero.

At the 1988 Olympic Games in Seoul, South Korea, Lewis ran second to Ben Johnson, who won the 100-metre event in record time. Lewis was awarded the gold medal soon afterward when Johnson was found to have used steroids. Lewis earned a second gold in Seoul for the long jump, but his continued success did little to improve his popularity.

By 1992 Lewis had won eight world championship gold medals and had owned the long jump for ten years. Age began to take its toll on him, however. At the 1992 Olympics, Lewis experienced something that he had never received—total acceptance from an American crowd. He was given a standing ovation in New Orleans, Louisiana, as his second-place finish in the long jump qualified him for an Olympic berth. The admiration of fans came showering down in Barcelona, Spain, in 1992, when Lewis beat Powell in the long jump to earn his seventh gold medal and then anchored the 400-metre relay for his eighth.

Following the 1992 Olympics, Lewis's performance began to decline, and by 1995 he was being beaten regularly by younger athletes. Still, Lewis participated in the 1996 Olympic trials and won a chance to compete in the long jump at the games in Atlanta,

Georgia. He easily won his fourth straight gold in the event. Endorsement contracts came from Panasonic, among others, and large personal appearance fees.

In 1999 Lewis was named as one of the century's greatest athletes at the Sports Illustrated 20th Century Sports Awards ceremony. In December 2001 Lewis was elected to the National Track and Field Hall of Fame. He also tried acting, appearing in the 2002 television movie *Atomic Twister.*

Eight of Lewis's Olympic gold medals are still in his possession. The ninth—his first, for the 100-meter sprint—was buried with his father Bill in May of 1988. Lewis revealed in the *Philadelphia Daily News,* "More than anything, he wanted me to win that medal.... Now he has it and he'll always have it."

❖❖❖

66
Abraham Lincoln
(1809-1865)

Abraham Lincoln was the 16th president of the United States. He preserved the Union during the American Civil War and brought about the emancipation of the slaves. He became the first American president to be assassinated. He was the first Republican president

Lincoln was born in Hardin County, Kentucky on February 12, 1809.

When he was seven, the family moved to southern Indiana. As he grew up, he loved to read. He was constantly borrowing books from the neighbours.

Lincoln moved to New Salem, Illinois, where he lived until 1837. While there he worked at several jobs including operating a store, surveying, and serving as postmaster. He impressed the residents with his character, wrestled the town bully, and earned the nickname "Honest Abe".

Lincoln saw brief service in the Black Hawk War, and he made an unsuccessful run for the Illinois legislature in 1832. He ran again in 1834, 1836, 1838, and 1840, and he won all four times. Additionally, he studied law in his spare time and became a lawyer in 1836.

In 1846 Lincoln ran for the United States House of Representatives and won. While in Washington he became known for his opposition to the Mexican War and to slavery. He returned home after his term and resumed his law practice more seriously than ever.

Lincoln's declining interest in politics was renewed by the passage of the Kansas-Nebraska Act in 1854. He made an unsuccessful bid for the U.S. Senate but received some support for the Republican vice-presidential nomination in 1856. Also, in 1856 Lincoln gave his Lost Speech. He opposed the Dred Scott decision in 1857 and gave his famous "House Divided" Speech on June 16, 1858. Additionally, he engaged in a series of debates with Stephen A. Douglas in 1858. Lincoln was against the spread of slavery into the territories but was not an abolitionist. Douglas won the Senatorial race, but Lincoln gained national recognition. In 1860 he furthered his national reputation with a successful speech at the Cooper Institute in New York.

In 1860, Lincoln was elected the 16th president on November 6, 1860. After his election, many Southern states, fearing Republican control in the government, seceded from the Union. After the fall of Ft. Sumter, Lincoln raised an army and decided to fight to save the Union from falling apart. He stuck with this pro-Union policy for four long years of Civil War. On January 1, 1863, the Emancipation Proclamation went into effect. This was Lincoln's declaration of freedom for all slaves in the areas of the Confederacy not under Union control. Also, on November 19, 1863, he gave his famous Gettysburg Address which dedicated the battlefield there to the soldiers who had perished. He called on the living to finish the task the dead soldiers had begun.

Lincoln's domestic policies included support for the Homestead Act. This act allowed poor people in the East to obtain land in the West. Also, Lincoln signed legislation entitled the National Banking Act which established a national currency and provided for the creation of a network of national banks. In addition, he signed tariff legislation that offered protection to American industry and signed a bill that chartered the first transcontinental railroad. Lincoln's foreign policy was geared toward preventing foreign intervention in the Civil War.

In 1864 Ulysses S. Grant was named general-in-chief of the armies of the United States. The South was slowly being worn down. Lincoln was reelected president with Andrew Johnson as his running mate. On April 9, 1865, General Robert E. Lee surrendered to Grant. Two days later Lincoln addressed a crowd outside the White House. Among other things, he suggested he would support voting rights for certain blacks. This infuriated a racist and Southern sympathizer who was in the audience: the actor John Wilkes Booth who hated everything the president stood for.

On Good Friday, April 14, 1865, the Lincolns attended a play entitled *Our American Cousin* at Ford's Theatre. During the performance Booth shot the president in the back of his head at about 10:15 pm. Lincoln was carried across the street to the Petersen House where he passed away the next day at 7:22 am. This was the first presidential assassination in American history, and the nation mourned its leader.

He was buried in the Lincoln Tomb in Oak Ridge Cemetery on May 4, 1865.

❖❖❖

67

Nelson Mandela

(1918-)

Nelson Rolihlahla Mandela is the first President of South Africa to be elected in a fully representative democratic election. The South African courts convicted him on charges of sabotage, as well as other crimes committed while he led the movement against apartheid. In accordance with his conviction, Mandela served 27 years in prison.

Nelson Rolihlahla Mandela was born on 18 July 1918 in Transkei, South Africa.

He completed his schooling at Headtown, a Wesleyan secondary school. He attended the University College of Fort Hare and studied for the Bachelor of Arts Degree. He was soon elected onto the Student's Representative Council. He took part in a protest and was suspended from the college.

Four years later he graduated from Healdtown, and left to pursue higher education at the University of Fort. It was here he first met his lifelong friend and associate Oliver Tambo.

It was in 1942, while he was studying for his law degree, that he joined the ANC (African National Congress).

During the latter years of World War II, Nelson Mandela and members of the ANC, like Walter Sisulu, Oliver Tambo and Anton Lembede, started to devise plans to transform the politically polite ANC movement into a rolling mass movement. They spread the message of liberation to the people living in townships and in the rural areas. These young men formed the African National Congress Youth League (ANCYL) in 1944 and three years later, Nelson was elected as Secretary of the league. He rose quickly and steadily in the ranks and spearheaded many active campaigns to peacefully bring about an end to racism and compulsory education for all children.

In 1949, The Programme of Action, inspired by the Youth League, which advocated the weapons of boycott, strike, civil disobedience and non-co-operation was accepted as official ANC policy. After the 1948 election victory of the Afrikaner-dominated National Party, with its apartheid policy of racial segregation, Mandela was prominent in the ANC's 1952 Defiance Campaign and the 1955 Congress of the People, whose adoption of the Freedom Charter provided the fundamental programme of the anti-apartheid cause.

Initially committed to non-violent mass struggle and acquitted in the marathon Treason Trial of 1956-1961, Mandela and his colleagues accepted the case for armed action after the shooting of unarmed protesters at Sharpeville, in March 1960, and the banning of anti-apartheid groups. In 1961, he became the commander of the ANC's armed wing, Umkhonto we Sizwe. In August of the following year, he was arrested and jailed for five years. In June 1964 he was sentenced again, this time to life imprisonment, for his involvement in planning armed action.

He started his prison years in the infamous Robben Island Prison, a maximum security facility on a small island off the coast of Cape Town. In April 1984, he was transferred to Pollsmoor Prison in Cape Town and in December 1988 he was moved the Victor Verster Prison near Paarl from where he was eventually released.

Mandela remained in prison until February 1990, when sustained ANC campaigning and international pressure led to his release. On 2 February 1990, South African President F.W. de Klerk lifted the ban on the ANC and other anti-apartheid organisations. Mandela was released from Victor Verster Prison on 11 February 1990.

He and President de Klerk - who did much to dismantle the institutions of apartheid - shared the Nobel Peace Prize in 1993. In Mandela's 1994 autobiography, *Long Walk to Freedom,* he did not reveal anything about the alleged complicity of de Klerk in the violence of the 1980s and 90s, or the role of his ex-wife Winnie Mandela in that bloodshed. However, he later discussed those issues in *Mandela: The Authorised Biography.*

Between 1990 and 1994, Mandela led the party in the multi-party negotiations that led to the country's first multi-racial elections. As the first black president of South Africa (1994-1999), he presided over the transition from minority rule and apartheid.

After his retirement as President in 1999, Mandela went on to become an advocate for a variety of social, and human-rights organisations. He continues travelling the world, meeting leaders, attending conferences and collecting awards.

68
Lata Mangeshkar
(1929-)

Lata Mangeshkar is one of the best-known playback singers in the Hindi film industry. She is listed in the Guinness Book of World Records as the most recorded artist in the world. She has sung in more than 20 languages. Also known as the Nightingale of India, she is the recipient of the Bharat Ratna, Padma Vibhushan, Padma Bhushan and other prestigious awards.

Lata was born on September 28, 1929 in Indore, Madhya Pradesh.

At a very early age of 4, she was introduced to classical music by her stage actor-singer father. When she was five years old, she began working as a theatre artist in sangeet nataks.

Lata sang her maiden cinematic song for the Marathi film *Kiti Hasaal* (1942). Her father did not like her singing for films. So, her song was deleted from the movie. In the year 1942, after his demise, the responsibility of the family fell on her shoulders and at the age of 13, she was compelled to act with the help of Master Vithal, doing films like *Pahili Mangalagaur, Majhe Baal, Gaja Bhau* and Hindi films like *Badi Maa, Jeevan Yatra* and *Samudra Mandir*.

It was in 1945 that this celestial voice caught the fancy of millions of Hindi music lovers, and in 1949 she sang songs for films like *Mahal, Baiju Bawara, Nagin, Madhumati*, etc. She got her biggest break, when she sang "Aayega Aanewaala" for the movie *Mahal*. The song was a hit.

She stepped in when the Bollywood music scene was dominated by the legendary Shamshad Begum and Noorejahan. More than half a century later, that voice, still reigns supreme despite two generations of wannabes like Sharda, Hemlata, Suman Kalyanpur, Aarti Mukherjee, Anuradha Paudwal, Kavita Krishnamurthy, Alka Yagnik, etc. trying to take over from her.

The period of 1950s witnessed tremendous growth in her career. She worked with all the famous composers of that era, like Shankar Jaikishan, S D Burman, Naushad, Hemant Kumar, and Salil Chowdhury. Shankar Jaikishan were absolutely stunned by her voice and used her voice for playback singing in almost all the movies that they got.

She has continued surprising her fans with the range of her singing in films like *Dil Se, Zubeidaa* and most recently *One 2 Ka 4*.

She cut down on her work pressure in the 70's and got involved in her stage shows abroad from whence Raj Kapoor brought her back to sing for *Ram Teri Ganga Maili*. And then once again she made her grand comeback with *Chandni* and *Maine Pyaar Kiya, Lamhe, Dilwale Dulhaniya Le Jayenge, Darr, Yeh Dillagi*, and *Dil To Pagal Hai*.

Lata has also sung some non-film songs including ghazals with Jagjit Singh, Bengali songs with renowned music directors like Salil Chowdhury and Hemant Kumar. She has sung with famous singers like Mohammed Rafi, Kishore Kumar, Mukesh, Manna Dey, etc. She has perfected almost every genre of music.

She has been honoured with many awards: Maharashtra Bhushan Award, Dadasaheb Phalke award, National Awards plus Filmfare awards, Bharat Ratna, Padma Vibhushan, Padma Bhushan Lata Mangeshkar withdrew from the Filmfare awards to encourage newcomers in music. She has also won several Lifetime Achievement Awards (Filmfare, Star Screen, Zee

Cine, IIFA in London) and is recorded in the Guinness Book of World Records for having sung the maximum number of songs in the world.

She continues to sing every now and then for Hindi movies and performs live.

❖❖❖

69

Guglielmo Marconi

(1874-1937)

Marchese Guglielmo Marconi was an Italian inventor, best known for his development of a radiotelegraph system. He shared the 1909 Nobel Prize in Physics with Karl Ferdinand Braun in recognition of their contributions to the development of wireless telegraphy.

Guglielmo Marconi was born April 25, 1874, in Bologna.

He was educated by private tutors and attended the Livorno (Leghorn) technical institute for a short time.

In 1894 Marconi began experiments on electromagnetics near Bologna, directing his attention to the distance over which they could be detected with the possibility that they might be used in a telegraph. He repeated Heinrich Hertz's experiments and rapidly extended the range of detection.

Moving out of doors in 1895, he introduced a transmitter sparking between an elevated aerial and earth. For detection he used a "coherer", similarly connected between an aerial and earth. By the end of 1895 he was able to detect wireless signals at ranges greater than a mile and out of the line of sight. By interrupting the spark signal, he was able to transmit Morse code. He patented his invention in 1896.

Marconi, unable to interest the Italian government in wireless, went to England in 1896, where he received support from the

British Post Office. Ranges attained by his instrument rose quickly, to 8 miles and then 25 miles and more. In 1896, he sent messages across the Bristol Channel from Penarth, near Cardiff, to Weston-super-Mare. He afterwards set up installations of wireless telegraphy between the South Foreland and the East Goodwin light-vessel, the South Foreland and Wimereux in France, Harwich, and Chelmsford. In 1899 signals across the English Channel, between Boulogne and Dover, caused a sensation, though the distance was less than that covered by other transmissions. His system was definitely adopted by the Admiralty in 1900.

In 1900 Marconi determined to try sending wireless signals across the Atlantic, despite the theoretical conflict between rectilinear propagation of Hertz radiation and the curvature of the earth. He had, however, already received signals at 250-mile range. Using the Poldhu transmitter, an established station in southwestern England, and a temporary aerial supported by a kite on Signal Hill, St. John's, Newfoundland, nearly 1,800 miles away, he received the first transatlantic wireless signals on December 12, 1901.

Also in 1901 Marconi patented his "four-circuit" tuning system. Thus multiplex wireless telegraphy became possible, and the interference of one signal with another was minimized.

In 1902 Marconi patented a sensitive magnetic radio detector to replace the coherer and, in 1905, the horizontal directional aerial, which at once brought improvements in signal strengths and allowed the development of long-distance commercial wireless.

After 1905 Marconi spent much of his time as an entrepreneur, with a talented staff of engineers and administrators, developing wireless telegraphy. In 1907 commercial communication was established between Marconi stations at Clifden in western Ireland and Glace Bay, Nova Scotia.

During World War I Marconi began experiments on shortwave radio and on aerials designed to transmit along narrow beams to minimise detection by an enemy. The year 1917 saw him as a member of the Italian mission to the United States on its entry into the war, and in 1919 he was a signatory to the Paris Treaty for Italy.

He spent much of the next decade continuing the shortwave investigations begun in wartime, making useful discoveries, but none to compete with the great postwar expansion of the radio networks consequent on the development of radiotelephony and voice radio. In Britain, however, Marconi and his companies were influential in the startup of public radio broadcasting and help establish the British Broadcasting Company, later the British Broadcasting Corporation or BBC.

He shared the 1909 Nobel Prize for physics with K. F. Braun. He was made a noble with the rank of marchese in 1929.

Marconi died on July 20, 1937, in Rome of a heart attack.

❖❖❖

70
Karl Marx
(1818-1883)

Karl Heinrich Marx was a German philosopher, political economist, historian, sociologist, humanist, political theorist and revolutionary credit70

Karl Marx was born in Trier, Germany, on May 5, 1818.

After schooling in Trier, he was educated in the best universities in Germany at Bonn, Berlin and Jena. He was greatly influenced by Georg Wilhelm Friedrich Hegel.

He moved to Cologne where the city's liberal opposition movement was fairly strong. Known as the Cologne Circle, this group had its own newspaper, *The Rhenish Gazette.* The newspaper published an article by Marx where he defended the freedom of the press. The group was impressed by the article and in October, 1842, Marx was appointed editor of the newspaper

Here he met Moses Hess, a radical who called himself a socialist. Marx began attending socialist meetings organised by Hess. Based on what he heard at these meetings, Marx wrote an article for *The Rhenish Gazette* in January 1843 on the poverty of the Mosel wine-farmers and was also critical of the government. The newspaper was banned by the Prussian authorities.

Warned that he might be arrested, Marx quickly moved to France where he was offered the post of editor of a new political journal,

Franco-German Annals. In Paris he began mixing with members of the working class for the first time. He was shocked by their poverty but impressed by their sense of comradeship. In an article that he wrote for the Franco-German Annals he argued that the working class would eventually be the emancipators of society. When published in February 1844, the journal was immediately banned in Germany. Marx also upset the owner of the journal, Arnold Ruge, who objected to his editor's attack on capitalism.

In 1844 Marx wrote *Economic and Philosophic Manuscripts*. In this work he developed his ideas on the concept of alienation. While in Paris he became a close friend of Friedrich Engels, who shared Marx's views on capitalism. Marx and Engels decided to work together. Marx was at his best when dealing with difficult abstract concepts, and Engels had the ability to write for a mass audience. While working on their first article together, "The Holy Family", on 25 January 1845, Marx received an order deporting him from France. Marx and Engels decided to move to Belgium, a country that permitted greater freedom of expression than any other European state.

Engels gave Marx the royalties of his recently published book, *Condition of the Working Class in England* and arranged for other sympathizers to make donations. This enabled Marx the time to study and develop his economic and political theories.

In January 1846 Marx set up a Communist Correspondence Committee. The plan was to try and link together socialist leaders living in different parts of Europe. Marx formed a branch in Brussels and in December 1847 attended a meeting of the Communist League' Central Committee in London. At the meeting it was decided that the aims of the organisation was "the overthrow of the bourgeoisie, the domination of the proletariat, the abolition of the old bourgeois society based on class antagonisms, and the establishment of a new society without classes and without private property".

When Marx returned to Brussels he concentrated on writing *The Communist Manifesto*. Based on a first draft produced by Friedrich Engels called the *Principles of Communism*, Marx finished the 12,000 word pamphlet in six weeks. Unlike most of Marx's work, it was an accessible account of communist ideology. Written for a mass audience, the book summarised the forthcoming revolution and the nature of the communist society that would be established by the proletariat. *The Communist Manifesto* was published in February, 1848. The following month, the government expelled Marx from Belgium. Marx and Engels visited Paris before moving to Cologne where they founded a radical newspaper, the *New Rhenish Gazette*.

After examples of police brutality in Cologne, Marx helped establish a Committee of Public Safety to protect the people against the power of the authorities. *The New Rhenish Gazette* continued to publish reports of revolutionary activity all over Europe, including the Democrats seizure of power in Austria and the decision by the Emperor to flee the country.

On 9 May, 1849, Marx received news he was to be expelled from the country. The last edition of the *New Rhenish Gazette* appeared on 18 May and was printed in red. Marx wrote that although he was being forced to leave, his ideas would continue to be spread until the "emancipation of the working class".

In 1852, Charles Dana, the socialist editor of the *New York Daily Tribune*, offered Marx the opportunity to write for his newspaper. Over the next ten years the newspaper published 487 articles by Marx. Another radical in the USA, George Ripley, commissioned Marx to write for the *New American Cyclopaedia*.

Marx published *A Contribution to the Critique of Political Economy* in 1859 in which he argued that the superstructure of law, politics, religion, art and philosophy was determined by economic forces.

In England he devoted his life to researching his book on economics and history, *Das Kapital*. This was published in four volumes, only one of which came out during his life-time. The book dealt with important concepts such as surplus value; division of labour, industrial reserve army and the issue of revolution.

Marx, who had a swollen liver, died on 14 March, 1883.

❖❖❖

71

Zubin Mehta

(1936-)

Zubin Mehta is an Indian conductor of Western classical music. He has been honoured with the Order of the Lotus from India, the Médaille d'Or Vermeil (gold medal, from the city of Paris, and an appointment as Commendatore (Commander/Knight) by the Italian government.

Zubin Mehta was born in Bombay, India, in 1936.

Zubin studied piano and violin as a child, and at the age of sixteen he conducted his first orchestra rehearsal.

In 1954, he went to Vienna to study at the world-renowned Academy of Music. Here he learned to play the double bass from Otto Ruhm, and studied conducting with Hans Swarowsky, a pupil of the composer Richard Strauss. He received additional training in conducting from Carlo Zecchi and Alceo Galliera, both at the Accademia Musicale Chigiana in Siena, Italy.

After graduating from the Vienna Academy of Music in 1957, he made his conducting debut with the Tonkünstler Orchestra in Vienna's Musikverein. He won first place in the Liverpool International Conductors' Competition in England in 1958; this brought him a one-year assistant conducting position there.

In 1961, he was appointed music director of the Montreal Symphony Orchestra; shortly thereafter, he accepted a position as associate conductor of the Los Angeles Philharmonic. He turned both ensembles into first-class symphonies, raising ticket sales and visibility. When he assumed the directorship of the Los Angeles Philharmonic in 1962, he became the youngest conductor at that time to simultaneously lead two major orchestras.

Zubin made his debut as an opera conductor with Tosca in Montreal in 1964. In 1965, he made his Metropolitan Opera debut conducting Aida, followed by conducting opera at the Vienna State Opera, Florence, La Scala Milan, and, in 1977, at the Royal Opera House, Covent Garden, and the opera houses of Montreal, Chicago and Florence as well as at the Salzburg Festival.

He has enjoyed a long association with the Israel Philharmonic Orchestra. He was named as its music advisor in 1969, appointed music director in 1977, and in 1981, made music director for life.

Zubin left the Los Angeles Philharmonic in 1978 to take up the baton as conductor of the New York Philharmonic, a position he held until 1991. Critics and audiences were thrilled that a dynamic conductor known for his interpretations of late Romantic works would replace the ascetic, hyper-modern Pierre Boulez.

Since 1986, he has been the music advisor and conductor of the Italian summer festival Maggio Musicale Fiorentino. He has been Music Director of the Bavarian State Opera and the Bavarian State Orchestra from 1998 to 2006.

Zubin Mehta's list of awards and honours is extensive the "Nikisch-Ring" from the Vienna Philharmonic as well as having been made, in 2001, an honorary member of the orchestra. He was made an honorary member of the Vienna State Opera in 1997. In 1999 he was presented the "Lifetime Achievement Peace and Tolerance Award" of the United Nations by Lea Rabin. In April 2001 President Chirac created him "Chevalier de la Legion d'Honneur". In January 2004 the Munich Philharmonic Orchestra bestowed the title of "Honorary Conductor" on him. He is also the recipient of Padma Bhushan (India), Medaille d'Or Vermeil (Paris), and Commandre des Arts et des Lettres (France); honorary degrees from Tel Aviv University, Weizmann Institute of Science, Princeton University, Westminster Choir College, Hebrew

University, Jewish Theological Seminary, Brooklyn College, and Colgate University.

Mehta's recordings include the major works of the orchestral and operatic repertoire as well as collaborations with the phenomenally popular Three Tenors: Luciano Pavarotti, Placido Domingo, and José Carreras.

❖❖❖

72
Yehudi Menuhin
(1916-1999)

Yehudi Menuhin was born a U.S. citizen, but became a citizen of Switzerland in 1970, and of the United Kingdom in 1985. He was a violinist and conductor who had one of the longest and most distinguished careers of any violinist of the 20th century.

Yehudi Menuhin was born on April 22, 1916 in New York City.

Because he exhibited a precocious interest in music, Menuhin's parents granted his request for a violin, and he began studying in the San Francisco area, first with Sigmund Anker and then with San Francisco Symphony Orchestra concertmaster Louis Persinger. His first professional appearance came at the age of seven, at Oakland Auditorium in Oakland, California.

Sidney Ehrman, a San Francisco lawyer and philanthropist, was so taken by Menuhin's musical talent, and by that of his sisters Yaltah and Hephzibah, that he volunteered to pay for the family's expenses in order for the children to pursue their musical careers. His generosity allowed the family to go to Europe, where he studied with the violinist Georges Enesco; the family followed Enesco back to the U.S. in 1927.

It was that year that Menuhin made his Carnegie Hall debut, an appearance that launched him to instant stardom. He was a sensation—a mere boy of ten playing "grown up" concertos by Beethoven and Brahms with a mature understanding of the music that left observers breathless. After a concert he gave in Berlin in 1929, a wild-haired man approached him, embraced him, and exclaimed: "Now I know there is God in heaven!" The man was Albert Einstein.

During the 1930s Menuhin continued to give concerts, pursued a burgeoning recording career, and went on his first world performing tour, in 1935. During World War II he gave hundreds of concerts for Allied soldiers and relief organisations. He was the first foreign musician to perform in liberated Paris, and he played for prisoners who were awaiting liberation from the Bergen-Belsen concentration camp.

In 1959 Menuhin took up residence in England, and in 1962, he founded the Yehudi Menuhin School in Surrey, where intensive musical instruction is combined with traditional elementary and high school classes. Carrying on his role as a world citizen, he has championed jazz and non-Western music, performing with musicians such as Indian sitarist Ravi Shankar and French jazz violinist Stephane Grappelli.

Menuhin has been the recipient of the Nehru Award for Peace and International Understanding (India), Canadian Music Council Gold Medal, Kennedy Center Honor, Brahms Medal, Ordre des Arts et des Lettres (France), Legion d'honneur (France), Croix de Lorraine (France), Order of Merit (Germany); honorary knighthood from Queen Elizabeth II, 1965.

From 1959 he lived in London, but he did not become a British citizen until 1985.

Menuhin died of a heart attack on March 12, 1999, in Berlin, Germany, where he had travelled to conduct the Warsaw Symphony Orchestra.

73

Michelangelo

(1475-1564)

Michelangelo di Lodovico Buonarroti Simoni was an Italian Renaissance painter, sculptor, architect, poet and engineer. Titian and Venetian painting generally was very much influenced by his vision, and he is responsible in large measure for the development of Mannerism.

Michelangelo was born on March 6, 1475 at Caprese in Casentino, Italy.

Michelangelo's desire to become an artist was initially opposed by his father. He was, however, eventually apprenticed in 1488 for a three-year term to Domenico Ghirlandaio. Here he learnt the rudiments of the technique of fresco painting.

Before the end of his apprenticeship, however, he transferred to the school set up by Lorenzo the Magnificent in the gardens of the Palazzo Medici. During this time, Michelangelo painted *Madonna of the Steps* (1490-1492) and *Battle of the Centaurs* (1491-1492).

With the death of Lorenzo in 1492, the school broke up and Michelangelo was given permission to study anatomy at the hospital attached to Sto Spirito. In gratitude to the prior for allowing him this privilege he carved a wooden Crucifix (the one in the Casa Buonarroti).

In October 1494, Michelangelo transferred to Bologna and was awarded the commission for three marble figures to complete the tomb of St. Dominic begun by the deceased Niccoló dell' Arca.

By June 1496 he was in Rome and here established his reputation with two marble statues, the drunken Bacchus (c 1496-7; Florence, Bargello) for a private patron and the Pietá for St. Peter's (1498-9). The latter is generally considered to be the masterpiece of his early years, the perfect union of Christian emotion with classical form, deeply poignant, exquisitely beautiful and more highly finished than his later works were to be.

He returned to Florence a famous sculptor and was awarded the commission for the colossal figure of David, symbol of resistance and independence, to stand in the Piazza della Signoria, flanking the entrance to the Palazzo Vecchio (1501-4, original now in the Accademia). This work finally established his reputation as a sculptor extraordinaire.

Soon after this he was commissioned to paint a battle scene for the new Council Chamber of the Palazzo. On one wall he commenced the painting of the Battle of Cascina, while on the opposite wall his principal rival, Leonardo, was commissioned to paint the Battle of Anghiari. Although neither painting was ever finished, copies of a fragment of Michelangelo's full-size cartoon, showing a group of nude soldiers reacting variously to the battle alarm that has interrupted their bathing, soon began to circulate. These nudes, posed in a variety of turning and animated poses, established the Mannerist conception of the male nude as the principal vehicle for the expression of human emotions.

Michelangelo abandoned this Florentine commission when Pope Julius II summoned him to Rome to design his tomb. What should have been the most prestigious commission of his career, a free-standing tomb with some 40 figures, to be located in St. Peter's, became, in Michelangelo's own words, the 'tragedy of the tomb'. Julius died in 1513, the contract was redrawn several times over the following years with ever-diminishing funding, other demands were made on Michelangelo by successive popes, and the project was finally cobbled together in 1545, a shadow of its original conception, with much help from assistants, in S. Pietro in Vincoli Julius's titular church. The tomb is now principally famous for the colossal figure of Moses (c 1515), one of Michelangelo's greatest sculptures,

Two slave figures, *The Dying Slave* and the *Rebellious Slave* (c1513), intended for the largest of the schemes for the tomb, are now in the Louvre in Paris, and four unfinished slaves, are now in the Accademia in Florence. While in the early stages of work on the Tomb, Julius also commissioned Michelangelo to paint the ceiling of the Sistine Chapel. Michelangelo was evidently reluctant to abandon his sculptural project for one of painting, but he none the less began work in 1508, completed the first half by 1510 and the whole ceiling by 1512. In his sonnet *On the Painting of the Sistine Chapel,* he described all the discomforts involved in painting a ceiling. Always heralded as the supreme example of Florentine disegno, the recent restoration has also revealed Michelangelo to have been a brilliant colourist.

In 1516, the new pope, Leo X commissioned Michelangelo to design a facade for San Lorenzo, the Medici parish church in Florence. The commission came to nothing, but this unfulfilled scheme led to his two earliest architectural masterpieces, the Medici Chapel (or New Sacristy) attached to San Lorenzo and the Laurentian Library.

In 1534 Michelangelo departed for Rome, never to return to Florence. Soon after his arrival Pope Clement VIII commissioned him to paint the fresco of the Last Judgment for the Sistine Chapel. Michelangelo's fresco breathes the new militancy of the Catholic Counter-Reformation. The work was officially unveiled on 31 October 1541.

Following the Last Judgment Paul III commissioned from Michelangelo his two last major frescos for the Capella Paolina, the *Conversion of St. Paul* and the *Martyrdom of St. Peter* (1542-50). The same troubled spirit imbues Michelangelo's sculpture from this time, the *Pietá* (now Florence, Cathedral Museum), intended for his own tomb shows himself as Nicodemus - again, a comparison with the St. Peter's Pietá is eloquent testimony to the spiritual uncertainty of these later years.

Michelangelo's crowning achievements, however, were architectural. In 1537-39, he received a commission to reshape the Campidoglio, the top of Rome's Capitoline Hill, into a square. Although not completed until long after his death, the project was carried out essentially as he had designed it. In 1546, Michelangelo was appointed architect to St. Peter's. The cathedral was constructed according to Donato Bramante's plan, but Michelangelo became ultimately responsible for its dome and the exterior of the altar end of the building.

He continued in his last years to write poetry, and carved the two extraordinary, haunting and pathetic Late Pietas. He was wokring on one of them, The *Rondanini Pieta* in Milan, just 6 days before his death.

The artist died on 18 February 1564 at the age of 89 and was buried in Florence, according to his wishes.

❖❖❖

74

Wolfgang Amadeus Mozart

(1756-1791)

Wolfgang Amadeus Mozart was an Austrian composer whose mastery of the whole range of contemporary instrumental and vocal forms - including the symphony, concerto, chamber music, and especially the opera - was unrivalled in his own time and perhaps in any other.

Wolfgang Amadeus Mozart was born on January 27, 1756, in Salzburg.

His father, a noted composer and pedagogue, was then in the service of the archbishop of Salzburg. Mozart received such intensive musical training that by the age of 6 he was a budding composer and an accomplished keyboard performer. He toured Europe with his father and sister when he was seven, visiting, among other cities, London and Paris.

In 1762 and 1768 he played to Maria Theresia at Schönbrunn. He spent the years 1766-1769 at Salzburg writing instrumental works and music for school dramas in German and Latin, and in 1768 he produced his first real opera: the German *Singspiel* (that is, with spoken dialogue) *Bastien und Bastienne* and the opera *buffa La finta semplice.* He composed numerous symphonies, concertos, and divertimenti, as well as much chamber and keyboard music.

In Italy, Mozart was well received: at Milan. He obtained a commission for an opera; at Rome he was made a member of an honorary knightly order by the Pope; and at Bologna the Accademia Filarmonica awarded him membership. He produced his first large-scale settings of opera seria (that is, court opera on serious subjects): *Mitridate (*1770), *Ascanio in Alba* (1771), and *Lucio Silla* (1772), as well as his first *String Quartets*.

At Salzburg in late 1771 he renewed his writing of *Symphonies (Nos. 14-21)*. In this period at Salzburg (1773-1777) he wrote nine *Symphonies (Nos. 22-30)*, including the excellent *No. 29* in A Major; a large number of divertimenti, including the *Haffner Serenade*; all of his six *Concertos* for violin, several other concertos, and church music for use at Salzburg.

After nine difficult months in Paris, from March 1778 to January 1779, Mozart returned once more to Salzburg. He wrote music, again mainly for wind instruments: the *Sinfonia Concertante* for four solo wind instruments and orchestra, the *Concerto* for flute and harp, other chamber music, and the ballet music *Les Petits riens*. In addition, he was compelled to give lessons to make money. He concentrated on instrumental music *(Symphony Nos. 32-34)*, the *Symphonie Concertante* for violin and viola, several orchestral divertimenti, and (despite the lack of a theatre) an unfinished German opera, later called *Zaide*.

In 1780 Mozart received a long-awaited commission from Munich for the opera seria *Idomeneo*, musically one of the greatest of his works despite its unwieldy libretto and one of the great turning points in his musical development as he moved from his peregrinations of the 1770s to his Vienna sojourn in the 1780s. *Idomeneo* is, effectively, the last and greatest work in the entire tradition of dynastic opera seria, an art form that was decaying at the same time that the great European courts were themselves beginning to sense the winds of social and political revolution. Mozart's only other work in this genre, the opera seria *La clemenza di Tito* (1791), was a hurriedly written work composed on demand for a coronation at Prague - not cast in the traditional large dimensions of old-fashioned opera seria, with its long arias, but cut to two acts like an opera.

Mozart's years in Vienna, from age 25 to his death at 35, encompass one of the most prodigious developments in so short a span in the history of music. But in these 10 years Mozart's music grew rapidly beyond the comprehension of many of his contemporaries; it exhibited both ideas and methods of elaboration that few could follow, and to many the late Mozart seemed a difficult composer. The major instrumental works of this period encompass all the fields of Mozart's earlier activity and some new ones: six symphonies, including the famous last three: *No. 39* in E-flat Major, *No. 40* in G Minor, and *No. 41* in C Major (the Jupiter-a title unknown to Mozart). He finished these three works within six weeks during the summer of 1788, a remarkable feat even for him.

In the field of the string quartet Mozart produced two important groups of works that completely overshadowed any he had written before 1780: in 1785 he published the six *Quartets* dedicated to Haydn and in 1786 added the single *Hoffmeister Quartet.* In 1789 he wrote the last three *Quartets,* dedicated to King Frederick William of Prussia, a noted cellist.

Other chamber music on the highest level of imagination and craftsmanship from Mozart's Vienna years includes the two *Piano Quartets,* seven late *Violin Sonatas,* the last *Piano Trios,* and the *Piano Quintet* with winds; and in the last five years of his life, the last *String Quintets* and the *Clarinet Quintet.* This decade also saw the composition of the last 17 of Mozart's *Piano Concertos,* almost all written for his own performance. They represent the high point in the literature of the classical concerto, and in the following generation only Ludwig van Beethoven was able to match them. In his last opera, *The Magic Flute* (1791), Mozart turned back to German opera, and he produced a work combining many strands of popular theatre but with means of musical expression ranging from quasi-folk song to Italianate coloratura.

Mozart then turned to work on what was to be his last project, the *Requiem*. Ill and exhausted, he managed to finish the first two movements and sketches for several more, but the last three sections were entirely lacking when he died. It was completed by his pupil Franz Süssmayer after his death.

Mozart died on December 5, 1791.

❖❖❖

75

Prophet Muhammad

(ca. 570-632)

Mohammed was the founder of the religion of Islam. His life, teachings, and miracles have been the subjects of Muslim devotion and reflection ever since. He is regarded by Muslims as a messenger and prophet of God. He was also active as a diplomat, merchant, philosopher, orator, legislator, reformer, military general, and, according to Muslim belief, an agent of divine action.

Prophet Muhammad was born in 570 CE in Mecca.

Muhammad was orphaned soon after birth, and was brought up by his uncle Abu Talib. When he was 24, he married Khadija, a wealthy widow much his senior. Khadija's daughter Fatima was the only child of Muhammad to have issue. His position in the community was that of a wealthy merchant.

When he was 40, during the holy month of Ramajan, while he was sleeping in a mountaintop cave near Mecca, he received the first revelation of the *Qur'an,* a vision in which he was commanded by the angel Gabriel to preach. Belief in the inspiration given to Muhammad by the angel Gabriel during this dream is a fundamental element of Islam. According to Muhammad, he is the last prophet placed at the end of a long line of precursors, who had been inspired in the same way. Their inspiration, to which Islamic theology gives the name *Revelation,* was destined to be made public, and such inspiration ceased after Muhammad's death

Thereafter throughout his life, he continued to have revelations, many of which were collected and recorded in the *Qur'an.*

His fundamental teachings were: there is one God; people must in all things submit to Him; in this world nations have been amply punished for rejecting God's prophets, and heaven and hell are waiting for the present generation; the world will come to an end with a great judgment. He included as religious duties frequent prayer and almsgiving.

In his first years Muhammad made few converts but many enemies. His first converts were Khadija, Ali (who became the husband of Fatima), and Abu Bakr. From about 620, Mecca became actively hostile, since much of its revenues depended on its pagan shrine, the Kaaba, and an attack on the existing Arab religion was an attack on the prosperity of Mecca. While he was gaining only enemies at home, Muhammad's teaching was faring little better abroad; only at Yathrib did it make any headway, and on Yathrib depended the future of Islam. He preached his message here for nine years, attracting many disciples.

In 622 Muhammad fled from Mecca from an attempted murder and made his way to Yathrib. From this event, the flight, or *Hegira,* of the Prophet (622), the Islamic calendar begins.

Muhammad spent the rest of his life at Yathrib, henceforth called Medina, the City of the Prophet. At Medina he built his model theocratic state and from there ruled his rapidly growing empire. His lawgiving at Medina is at least theoretically the law of Islam, and in its evolution over the next 10 years the history of the community at Medina is seen.

Medina lies on the caravan route north of Mecca, and the Kuraishites of Mecca could not endure the thought of their outlawed relative taking vengeance on his native city by plundering their caravans. A pitched battle between Muhammad's men and the Meccans occurred at Badr, and the victory of an inferior force from the poorer city over the men of Mecca gave Islam great prestige in southwest Arabia. By this time pagan Arabia had been converted, and the Prophet's missionaries, or legates, were active in the Eastern Empire, in Persia, and in Ethiopia.

Muhammad expected that the Jews and Christians would welcome him and accept his revelations, but he was soon disappointed. Medina had a large Jewish population which controlled most of the wealth of the city, and they steadfastly refused to give their new ruler any kind of religious allegiance. Muhammad, after a long quarrel, appropriated much of their property, and his first actual conquest was the oasis of Khaibar, occupied by the Jews, in 628. The failure of several missions among the Christians made him distrustful of Christians as well as Jews.

His renown increased, and in 629 he made a pilgrimage to Mecca without interference. There he won valuable converts, including Amr and Khalid. In 630 he marched against Mecca, which fell without a fight. Arabia was won.

He died on June 8, 632.

Muslims throughout the world venerate Muhammad by expressing their love and devotion to him through numerous poems, folk songs, and formulaic prayers invoking God's blessings. His deeds and sayings are collected in the *sunna*. He was known to medieval Christianity as Mahomet.

❖❖❖

76

Guru Nanak

(1469-1539)

Sri Guru Nanak Dev is credited with starting the Sikh religion. He is worshipped next to God. His sole aim in life was to unify the Hindus and Muslims and form a universal religion of brotherhood and compassion.

Guru Nanak was born in Talwandi (now known as Nankana Sahib), on 20 October, 1469.

At the young age of five, Nanak began discussing on spiritual subjects. When he was seven years old, he went to a nearby school. In school, he picked up the wooden plank that served as his slate, and wrote on it an acrostic using all 35 letters of the Punjabi alphabet to compose verses that questioned the meaning of learning without understanding, a verse that forms part of the *Granth Sahib*. However, very soon, he left the school and started taking private classes. By the time he was 15, he had mastered Hindi, Persian, Punjabi and Sanskrit. As a young man herding the family cattle, Guru Nanak would spend long hours absorbed in meditation and in religious discussions with Muslim and Hindu holy men.

He studied Hinduism and Islam. He got married but then he abandoned his family and became an ascetic. While still a youth, he underwent a profound spiritual experience. For three days he disappeared, immersed in the river Baain. Here, says the *Puratan Janamasakhi*, he was in direct communion with God, who bade him to heed His words, and to carry them to all mankind.

Wandering for many years he came under the influence of both Hindus and Muslims (especially Sufi). Tradition states that he made four great journeys, travelling to all parts of India, and into Arabia and Persia; visiting Mecca and Baghdad. He spoke before Hindus, Jains, Buddhists, Parsees, and Muslims. He spoke in the temples and mosques, and at various pilgrimage sites. He visited many places to preach and spread his knowledge, which includes Burma, Iraq, Tibet and Sri Lanka.

It was during this period that Nanak met Kabir (1441-1518), a saint revered by both Hindus and Muslims, and who made a deep impression on him. Wherever he went, Guru Nanak spoke out against empty religious rituals, pilgrimages, the caste system, the practice of sati, of depending on books to learn the true religion, and of all the other tenets that were to define his teachings. Never did he ask his listeners to follow him. He asked the Muslims to be true Muslims and the Hindus to be true Hindus.

After the last of his great journeys, Guru Nanak settled in the town of Kartapur in Punjab on the banks of the Ravi where he taught for another 15 years. Followers from all over came to settle in Kartapur to listen, and sing, and be with him. Although his followers still remained of the religion to which they were born, they became known as the Guru's disciples, or Sikhs. It was here his followers began to refer to him as teacher, or guru. It was here that the Guru told his followers that they were to be householders and could not live apart from the world—there were to be no priests or hermits. He instituted the common meal (*langar*), requiring the rich and poor, Hindu and Muslim, high caste and low caste, to sit together while eating. It is here that Lehna, later to be Guru Angad, came to be with Guru Nanak.

He preached that God was omnipresent and did not adhere to any kind of ritualism or worship patterns. He led a life of purity and clarity and believed that the attainment of enlightenment would relieve one from the cycle of birth and death.

Guru Nanak composed a set of poems known as *Japji* that is recited as the Morning Prayer. It forms the first chapter of *Guru Granth Sahib*, the holy book of the Sikhs. These thoughts and poems inspire many till date and are considered the epitome of good living.

Guru Nanak passed away in 1539.

Just before Guru Nanak died, he called his disciples together and requested them to sing *Sohila*, the evening hymn. To satisfy both his Hindu and Muslim follower as to the funeral arrangements it is said he did not allow his body to remain behind.

❖❖❖

77

Jawaharlal Nehru

(1889-1964)

Jawaharlal Nehru, a politician and statesman of great skill, was one of the most important leaders of the Indian Independence Movement and, as the head of the Indian National Congress, became the first Prime Minister of India when India won its independence on August 15, 1947.

Jawaharlal Nehru was born on November 14, 1889, in Allahabad, India.

He was educated at home by, English and Scottish tutors. Under their influence he joined the Theosophical Society at 13.

At the age of 15 Nehru left for England. He was educated at Harrow and Trinity College, Cambridge. He later qualified as a barrister at the Inner Temple. He was called to the bar in 1912. His English experience reinforced his elegant and cosmopolitan tastes.

Back in India, Nehru began to practise law with his father. It was not until 1917 that Nehru was stirred by the imprisonment of Annie Besant, an Irish theosophist devoted to Indian freedom. As a result, Nehru became active in the Home Rule League. His involvement in the nationalist movement gradually replaced his legal practice.

Another great influence on him politically was Mohandas Gandhi, who educated much like Nehru in England, remained basically untouched, essentially Indian. He was very impressed by Gandhi's approach to Indian independence. A second issue which led him to join Gandhi was the Jallianwala massacre of 1919, in which some 400 Indians were shot on orders of a British officer.

In 1921 Nehru followed Gandhi in sympathy with the Khilafat cause of the Muslims. Nehru was drawn into the first civil disobedience campaign as general secretary of the United Provinces Congress Committee. The year 1921 also witnessed the first of Nehru's many imprisonments.

Nehru was immediately engrossed in party conferences and was elected president of the All-India Trades Union Congress. In 1928 he joined the radical opposition to proposals for dominion status by his father and Gandhi. In 1930 Gandhi supported Nehru as Congress president, attempting to divert radicalism from communism to the Congress.

In 1930 Nehru was arrested and imprisoned with his wife Kamala and Gandhi for violation of the Salt Law. From the end of 1931 to September 1935 Nehru was free for only six months.

During the 1937 elections the Muslim League offered to cooperate with the All-India Congress Committee in forming a coalition government in the United Provinces. Nehru refused, and the struggle between the Congress and the Muslim League was under way. Nehru also established the precedent for economic planning in a suggestion that the Congress form a national planning committee.

War in Europe drew India in, together with England. For Indian leaders the question was how an honourable settlement could be reached with England and still allow India to participate on the Allied side. Negotiations toward this end culminated in the Cripps mission and offer of dominion status in March 1942. Nehru refused to accept dominion status, as did the rest of Congress leadership. There followed the Congress "Quit India" resolution and the imprisonment of Nehru, Gandhi, and other Congress leaders until

June 1945. There were nationwide protests, a mass demand for independence.

In 1945, as Congress president, Nehru was pressed into negotiations with the Muslim League and the viceroy. These negotiations were marked by communal killings in Calcutta, followed by sympathetic outbreaks throughout India. Final decisions were reached between the last British viceroy, Lord Mountbatten, and Nehru, Gandhi, and Mohammad Ali Jinnah. Given his consistent opposition to the partition of India, his acceptance of the 3 June 1947 Plan, which created modern India and Pakistan, produced the outcome that he least desired. According to the Mountbatten Plan, two separate dominions were created. Nehru became prime minister and minister of external affairs of independent India in 1947.

He led the Congress to three successive general election victories (1952, 1957, and 1962) and following the death of Patel (1950) became the undisputed leader of the party.

Economic planning and welfare were the first claims on Nehru's attention. The Planning Commission was created in 1950 and Nehru launched the First Five-Year Plan in 1951, stressing an increase in agricultural output. He also took pride in the Community Development Programme, established to raise the standard of living in the villages.

He wrested Goa from the Portuguese. In 1954 he signed a Panchashila pact with China which asserted principles of peaceful coexistence and mutual non-aggression. These initiatives, however, could not prevent growing border tension between India and China which eventually erupted into a full-scale war in October 1962.

In 1955 he played a pre-eminent role at the Bandung Conference in Indonesia at which the Non-Aligned Movement was born. The following year Nehru visited USSR, followed by Khrushchev's visit to India which established strong economic ties between the two countries.

Nehru was a prolific writer. He wrote extensively during spells in prison. Among his more prominent works are *Glimpses of World History* (1935), *Autobiography* (1936), and the *Discovery of India* (1946).

He died on May 27, 1964, in New Delhi.

❖❖❖

78
Isaac Newton
(1643-172)

Sir Isaac Newton was an English physicist, mathematician, astronomer, natural philosopher, alchemist and theologian, and the greatest scientist of his era.

Isaac Newton was born on 4 January 1643 in Woolsthorpe, Lincolnshire.

Isaac went to the Free Grammar School and completed his school education in 1660.

In 1661, he went to Cambridge University where he became interested in mathematics, optics, physics and astronomy. He was especially strongly influenced by Euclid, although he was also influenced by Baconian and Cartesian philosophies.

In October 1665, a plague epidemic forced the university to close and Newton returned to Woolsthorpe. The two years he spent there were an extremely fruitful time during which he began to think about gravity, and also devoted time to optics and mathematics, working out his ideas about 'fluxions' (calculus).

In 1667, Newton returned to Cambridge, where he became a fellow of Trinity College. Two years later he was appointed second Lucasian Professor of Mathematics.

His first work as a Lucasian professor and understandably the topic of his first lecture course was optics. He reached the conclusion during the plague years that white light was not a simple entity. Most every other scholar thought it was, however the chromatic aberration in the lens of a telescope convinced Newton otherwise. Newton noticed that when a thin beam of sunlight was passed through a glass prism that a spectrum of colours were formed. He then presented the argument that white light is in actuality different types of rays which are refracted at different angles, which produces a different spectral colour. This prompted him to construct a refracting telescope. It was Newton's reflecting telescope, made in 1668, that finally brought him to the attention of the scientific community and in 1672 he was made a Fellow of the Royal Society.

From the mid-1660s, Newton conducted a series of experiments on the composition of light, discovering that white light is composed of the same system of colours that can be seen in a rainbow and establishing the modern study of optics.

However, in 1687, with the support of his friend the astronomer Edmond Halley, Newton published his single greatest work, the *Philosophiae Naturalis Principia Mathematica* (Mathematical Principles of Natural Philosophy), often shortened to *Principia Mathematica* or simply *The Principia*. This showed how a universal force, gravity, applied to all objects in all parts of the universe.

In 1689, Newton was elected MP for Cambridge University (1689-1690 and 1701-1702).

In 1696 he was appointed warden of the Royal Mint, settling in London. He took his duties at the Mint very seriously and campaigned against corruption and inefficiency within the organisation.

In 1703, he was elected president of the Royal Society, an office he held until his death. He was knighted by Queen Anne in 1705.

In 1704 Newton published *The Opticks* which dealt with light and colour. He also studied and published works on history, theology and alchemy.

He died on 31 March 1727 and was buried in Westminster Abbey.

❖❖❖

79

Florence Nightingale

(1820-1910)

Florence Nightingale, The Lady With the Lamp, was a British nursing hero of the Crimean War. She is also credited with as the English pioneer of data analysis and graphical presentation.

Florence Nightingale was born in Florence, Italy, on May 12, 1820.

In 1844 Nightingale decided to work in hospitals. Her family furiously resisted her plan. Nevertheless, she managed to do some private nursing and then to spend a few months at Kaiserworth, a German school and hospital.

In 1851 she received her initial training in Kaiserworth at a hospital run by an order of Protestant Deaconesses.

In 1853 she became superintendent of the London charity-supported Institution for Sick Gentlewomen in Distressed Circumstances. This opportunity allowed her to achieve effective independence from her family and also to try out novel techniques of institutional organisation and management, conducted in a scientific, non-sectarian spirit.

After reading a series of correspondence from the *London Times* in 1854 on the plight of wounded soldiers fighting in the Crimea, Nightingale asked the British secretary of war to secure her entrance into the military hospitals at Scutari, Turkey. He not only granted her permission but designated her as the head of an official delegation of nurses.

In October 1854 Nightingale organised a party of 38 nurses, mostly from various religious orders, for service in the Crimean War. They arrived at Constantinople in November. Conditions at the British base hospital at Scutari were appalling and grew steadily worse as the flow of sick and wounded soldiers from the Crimea rapidly increased. The medical services of the British army were both insufficient and inefficient: the Barrack Hospital, where Nightingale and her nurses were quartered, sat over a massive cesspool which poisoned the water and even the fabric of the building itself.

Nightingale worked for the next two years to improve the sanitary conditions of army hospitals and to reorganise their administration. She improved cleanliness, organisation, and cooking. The male orderlies who did the bulk of the actual nursing were smartened up, while Nightingale's private stores of clothing, bedding, and food enabled her to disregard army parsimony. She answered enquiries from kin and wrote condolences to families of common soldiers. Roving journalists and her family publicised her labours. *The Times* immortalised her as the "Lady with the Lamp" because she ministered to the soldiers throughout the night.

Nightingale conducted an exhaustive study of the health of the British Army and created a plan for reform that she compiled into a five-hundred-page report entitled *Notes on Matters Affecting the Health, Efficiency, and Hospital Administration of the British Army* (1858). In 1859 she published *Notes on Hospitals,* which was followed in 1860 by *Notes on Nursing: What It Is and What It Is Not.* That same year she established a nursing school at St. Thomas's Hospital in London.

Nightingale's huge cosmopolitan correspondence with eminent persons established female nursing and sanitary works as goals for nations. The International Red Cross appropriated her in the 1860s, despite her distrust of international conventions and supranational relief services. The world heroine had rendered her causes morally imperative and essential to national military power.

Florence Nightingale never really recovered from the physical strain of the Crimea. After 1861 she was house-bound and bedridden. She died on August 13, 1910.

❖❖❖

80

Pele

(1940-)

Edson (Edson) Arantes do Nascimento, best known by his nickname Pele, is a Brazilian former football player, who led the Brazilian national soccer team to three World Cup victories in 1958, 1962, and 1970 and to permanent possession of the Jules Rimet Trophy. He was given the title of Athlete of the Century by the International Olympic Committee.

Edson Arantes do Nascimento was born to a poor family on October 23, 1940, in Tres Coracoes, Brazil.

He first learned the game of soccer from his father, Dondinho, who was a centre forward until his career was halted by a fractured leg. Pele started training daily, but since he had no money to buy a real ball, he used a stuffed sock instead. After forming up a "shoeless team" with his street kids, Pele and his team participated in a youth tournament, with Pele ending up as top goal-scorer. He was immediately noticed by former Brazilian international Waldemar de Brito, who called him to the youth squad of Baquinho, whom he trained, and, for the first time, offered Pele money to play soccer. During his year at the club's youth team, Pele managed to win the championship after a dazzling performance: 148 goals in just 33 matches.

At just 15 years of age, Pele was bought by Brazil giants Santos, where he would later team up with some of Brazil's finest players of that era and future World Cup winners, such as Zito, Pepe or

Coutinho. Just one year later, he became the youngest player to start in the Brazilian first division at age 16, and even more incredibly, he became league top scorer at the end of the season. On his first appearance against Corinthians F.C., he scored a goal right away.

Pelé went on to play in four World Cups with Brazil's National Team. At the 1958 World Cup in Sweden, he stunned the world scoring six goals, including two in the championship game to help Brazil win its first World Cup 5-2 over Sweden. He was only 17 years-old, but a legend was born

In 1962 he played at in the finals in Chile, but an injury suffered in the first game of the tournament prevented him from helping Brazil win its second title.

At the 1970 finals in Mexico, the 29-year-old Pelé led one of the greatest teams ever assembled to win Brazil's third World Cup. In the 4-1 title triumph over Italy, Pelé, scored a glorious goal. It was Brazil's 100th World Cup goal, and the one he remembers the most.

One of the milestones in the history of Pele was definitely his 1000th goal scored in all competitions. On November 19, 1969, playing at the Maracana Stadium, Brazil's "cathedral of soccer", against arch-rivals Vasco Da Gama, he managed to score from a penalty kick and broke all records standing in front of him.

Pelé's statistics are staggering. During his career he scored 1,280 goals in 1,360 games, second only to another Brazilian, Arthur Friedenreich, who recorded 1,329 goals. He scored an average of a goal in every international game he played. Throughout his 15 years spent at the Brazil national team, Pele managed to break hundreds of records. He became the most prolific striker in Brazil's history, with 77 goals in 92 matches; scored 12 goals in different World Cup matches, being beaten only by Ronaldo. He is considered by FIFA the most prolific scorer in soccer history, with 1281 goals in 1363 matches in all competitions. He is the only player to have won three World Cups, although he did not receive a medal for the one in 1962, since he was injured in the final. He is one of the few players to achieve the performance of scoring in two different World Cup finals, sharing this record with Paul Breitner,

Vava and Zinedine Zidane. Pelé also holds the world record for hat tricks (92) and the number of goals scored on the international level (97).

He retired from the game in 1974, but came out of retirement the following year to play in the North American Soccer League for the New York Cosmos for just over two seasons. A reported 7-million-dollar contract for three years made him the highest paid soccer player of the North American Soccer League.

He published several best-selling autobiographies, starred in several documentary and semi-documentary films, and composed numerous musical pieces, including the entire sound track for the film *Pelé* (1977). He was the 1978 recipient of the International Peace Award, and in 1980 he was named Athlete of the Century. In 1993, he was inducted into the National Soccer Hall of Fame and is the former ambassador of sports in Brazil. In 2000, he was named second for the "Sportsman of the Century" award. The legendary Muhammad Ali got the honours. He has also done extensive work for children's causes through UNICEF.

81

Allah Rakha Rahman

(1967-)

Allah Rakha Rahman is an Indian film composer, record producer, musician and singer. He has won thirteen Filmfare Awards, four National Film Awards, a BAFTA Award, a Golden Globe and two Academy Awards.

Allah Rakha Rahman (named as A. S. Dileep Kumar at birth) was born on 6 January 1967 at Chennai, India.

Rahman started learning the piano at the age of four, and at the age of nine, his father passed away. Since the pressure of supporting his family fell on him, he joined Ilayaraja's troupe as a keyboard player at the age of 11. Infrequent attendance and an unaccommodative management forced him to shift schools from the prestigious Padma Seshadri Bal Bhavan to the Madras Christian College and finally he dropped out of school altogether.

He played on the orchestra of M.S.Vishwanathan and Ramesh Naidu and accompanied Zakir Hussain and Kunnakudi Vaidyanathan on world tours. All this experience enabled him to earn a scholarship to the famed Trinity College of Music at Oxford University from where he obtained a degree in Western Classical Music.

After he returned he continued to be a part of various music troupes. He was also a part of local rock bands like Roots, Magic and Nemesis Avenue where he performed with his future colleagues like Ranjit Barot and Sivamani. Vizi Manuel, the lead keyboard player in Illaiyaraja's troupe, advised him to try other alternatives like advertising. Fortunately for Rahman, he soon got his first break in advertising when he was asked to compose the jingle to promote Allwyn's new Trendy range of watches, in 1987. Thus began his five-year saga in advertising where he went on to compose more than 300 jingles. He did a lot of popular ads like those for Parry's, Leo Coffee, Boost, Titan, Premier Pressure Cooker, Hero Puch and Asian Paints. The jingles that he composed for the Leo Coffee ad starring Aravind Swamy and the Asian Paints ad directed by Rajeev Menon also won him awards and recognition. He also won an award for composing the theme music of the Madras Telugu Academy's Spirit of Unity Concerts.

In 1988, one of his sisters was seriously ill and numerous attempts to cure her failed. His family came in contact with a Muslim Pir and with his prayers and blessings, she made a miraculous recovery. Influenced by the teachings of the Pir, the entire family converted to Islam. Thus A.S. Dileep Kumar became Allah Rakha Rahman.

In 1989, he started a small studio called Panchathan Record Inn, which later developed into one of the most well-equipped and advanced sound recording studios in India.

At an advertising awards function, Rahman met one of India's most famous directors, Mani Ratnam. Rahman played him a few of his music samples. Mani loved them so much that he asked Rahman to compose the music for his next film, *Roja* (1992). The film won every conceivable award in music that year. Rahman also got the Rajat Kamal for best music director at the National Film Awards, the first time ever by a debutante. He moved into film music full time.

In the five years since *Roja,* he has created music for blockbuster Indian films including *Pudhiya Mugam, Gentleman, Kizhaku Seemaiyilae, Duet, Kadalan, Bombay, May, Madham, Indian, Muthu kadhal Dasam, Love Birds* and others. His 1995 soundtrack for *Bombay* crossed 5 million units and Rahman had arrived as the "King of Indian Pop" with sales of more than 40 million albums over a period of three years.

In the movie *Bombay* Rahman formally took to playback singing. He had lent his voice to bit pieces like in *Kadhalan* or background pieces and interludes like in *Roja*. But 'Hamma Hamma' in *Bombay* was Rahman's first complete song. His *Vandemataram* was a tribute to the motherland and featured songs to mark the three colours of the Indian Flag. It was released simultaneously in 28 countries across the world under the prestigious Columbia Label of Sony Music on August 15, 1997. Rahman himself performed live at Vijay Chowk in New Delhi on the eve of the Golden Jubilee of Indian Independence to a packed audience. The album was a mega success and sold over 1.2 million copies in India and did reasonably well internationally too.

He went on to compose several great hits for Tamil-language films before composing the score and songs for his first Hindi-language film, *Rangeela* (1995), followed by the chart-topping soundtrack albums of films such as *Bombay* (1995), *Dil Se* (1998), *Taal* (1999), *Zubeidaa* (2001), and *Lagaan* (2001), which was nominated for best foreign-language film at the 2002 Academy Awards.

At the age of 32, Rahman has already worked with internationally reputed artistes like Nusrat Fateh Ali Khan, Apache Indian, Zakir Hussain, Kunnakudi Vaidyanathan, Dominic Miller, L.Shankar, Kadri Gopalnath, Vikku Vinayakram, Ustad Sultan Khan and Pandit Vishwa Mohan Bhatt among many others. Rahman has in collaborations with artists such as L. Shankar, Zakir Hussain, David Byrne, Talvin Singh and Apache Indian - both recording and on tour.

He worked with Sir Andrew Lloyd Webber and Shekhar Kapoor on a musical called *Bombay Dreams*. He was nominated for a 2003 Laurence Olivier Theatre Award (The Hilton Award) for Best New Musical of 2002, *Bombay Dreams*, performed at the Apollo Theatre, West End, London, and on Broadway in New York City.

A R Rahman became the first Indian national to win a Golden Globe award at the 66th Golden Globe Award. He won the award for the film *Slumdog Millionaire* in the category of Best Original Score - motion picture. In 2009, *Slumdog Millionaire* fetched him

BAFTA Film Award in the category - best music, and Academy Awards in the category - best achievement in music written for motion pictures, and original score

AR Rahman is often referred to as the Mozart of Madras by his fans in India and abroad.

❖❖❖

82

Ramakrishna Paramahamsa

(1836-1886)

Ramakrishna was one of the most remarkable Indian saints of recent history. He is chiefly known for his high attainments in approaching God along many different paths.

Ramakrishna Paramahamsa was born Gadadhar Chattopadhyay on 18 February, 1836 in Kamarpukur, West Bengal.

Though Ramakrishna was very reluctant going to school, he had a God-gifted ability of painting and creating clay models. He loved nature so much that he used to spend much of his time in orchards and on the river-banks.

After the death of his father in 1843,Ramakrishna's elder brother Ramkumar was appointed as the chief-priest of the Dakshineswar temple by Rani Rasmoni, the founder of the temple. In 1852, Ramakrishna went to Calcutta and started assisting his brother at the same temple.

In 1856, after the death of Ramkumar, Ramakrishna took his place as the chief-priest of the temple. To him the deity of Kali was not a statue but the Mother herself and he carried out all the prescribed rites with full devotion and love for the Mother and an intense longing for a vision of her real form. She began to reveal herself to him, first in his trance states and later in ordinary consciousness. As his realisation deepened, the vision of the Mother became continuous.

In this phase of his spiritual journey, Ramakrishna saw God as the Divine Mother, but his spiritual journey was never static. Next he took up devotion to the form of the Avatar Rama who lived thousands of years ago and after attaining a vision of Rama, he next fixed his goal on Krishna, another divine incarnation. In this way Ramakrishna spent his whole life seeking God in many different ways.

One of his young charges had a *Bible* and used to read to Ramakrishna stories from it. He became enamoured of the wonderful stories of the life of Christ and of the beautiful picture of the Madonna with the Divine Child and fully immersed his mind in the Christian images for three days. On the fourth day as he was walking he saw an extraordinary looking person of serene aspect approaching him with his gaze intently fixed on him. Presently the figure drew near and from the inmost recesses of his heart there came the realisation. In his divine vision the Son of Man embraced him and became merged in him. He lost outward consciousness in Samadhi, realising his union with Brahman with attributes. Thus was he convinced that Jesus Christ was an Incarnation of the Lord.

In addition to being a Devotee, Ramakrishna also attained mergence in the Absolute. This came through a meeting with an advanced practitioner of Advaitha by the name of Totapuri who initiated him and taught him Advaitha philosophy. Then he asked Ramakrishna to withdraw the mind completely from all objects and dive into the Atman. Ramakrishna concentrated intensely and soared into the heights of *Nirvikalpa Samadhi*. Totapuri was astonished that Ramakrishna had attained in one day what it had taken him forty strenuous years to accomplish.

Sri Ramakrishna was the most 'rational mystic'. With scientific precision he put forward in most simple terms, as parables and stories, the eternal truth regarding God and God-realisation. To get rid of the thought that he belonged to a higher brahminical caste, he began to eat food cooked by the shudras or lower-caste.

At the age of eighteen, Sarada, the bride of the Ramakrishna, went to Dakshineshwar to join her husband. It was believed that the Ramakrishna regarded Sarada as the holy mother and she became his first disciple. Even after Ramakrishna's death in 1886, she led the movement and worked hard to make it a success.

Ramakrishna met Vivekananda for the first time in November 1881 when Vivekananda visited Dakshineswar to know if God really exists. In his reply Ramakrishna said, "Yes, I see God, just as I see you here, only in a much intenser sense. God can be realised." Vivekananda realised that Ramakrishna's words were honest and uttered from a deep experience. He started visiting Dakshineswar frequently and a relationship of "Master and disciple" developed between the two.

In 1885 Ramakrishna suffered from throat cancer. His condition worsened and on 16 August, 1886, he died at the Cossipore garden house.

After the death of Ramakrishna, the monastic disciples formed a fellowship headed by Vivekananda. This was the initial stage of Ramakrishna Mission. The Vedanta Society is an offshoot of Ramakrishna's and Vivekananda's work and publishes biographies and books of Vedantic knowledge relating to Ramakrishna.

❖❖❖

83

Chandrasekhara Venkata Raman

(1888-1970)

Sir Chandrasekhara Venkata Raman was an Indian physicist, recognised for his work on the molecular scattering of light and for the discovery of the Raman effect, which is named after him. He won the 1930 Nobel Prize in Physics and knighted in 1929. He awarded the Bharat Ratna in 1954.

Raman was born on 7 November 1888 at Thiruchirapall, India

At 11 years of age, he finished his secondary school education. When he was 15, he received B.A. with honours in Physics and English. He continued his studies at the Presidency College. In 1907, barely seventeen, he received his M.A. with honours. While he was student in the Presidency College, he modified 'Melde's theory on sound'. He also worked on 'Diffraction of Light'. His first paper appeared on this topic in 1906.

In 1907, after getting top ranking in the Financial Civil Service Competitive Exam, he was appointed as Deputy Accountant General in Calcutta. In 1915 he joined the Indian Science Association as a member and started his research work. In the year 1917, he resigned from his job and became the Professor of Physics at Calcutta University.

During a sea voyage to Europe in 1921, he observed with wonder the brilliant blue colour of the Mediterranean, and later the blue colour of glaciers. After returning to India he experimented on the diffusion of sunlight in its passage through water, transparent blocks of ice and other materials. He explained the reason of the blue colour of the ocean. Systematically pursuing his researches in this field, he was led to the discovery of 'Raman Effect' in 1928. He used monochromatic light from a mercury arc and the spectroscope to study the nature of diffused radiations emerging from the material under examination. For this discovery he was awarded Nobel Prize in 1930.

He was elected to the Royal Society of London in 1924 and knighted in 1929. The following year he was honoured with the prestigious Hughes Medal from the Royal Society. He won the Bharat Ratna award in 1954 and the Lenin Peace Prize in 1957.

He also worked in the field of magnetic attraction and theory of musical instruments. He continued as Professor for 15 years. He became president of the 16th session of the Indian Science Congress in 1929. In 1933, he became the Director of Indian Institute of Science, Bangalore. He held this post for 10 years. In 1934 he sponsored the foundation of the Indian Academy of Sciences, of which he became president.

In 1943, the Raman Research Institute was set up by him. Then he conducted research work for the rest of his life. He also started a company called Travancore Chemical and Manufacturing Co. Ltd. in 1943 along with Dr. Krishnamurthy. The Company during its 60 year history, established 4 factories in Southern India.

In 1947, he was appointed as the first National Professor by the new government of Independent India.

His publications include *Molecular Diffraction of Light, Mechanical Theory of Bowed Strings and Diffraction of X-rays, Theories of Musical Instruments*, etc.

Raman conducted pioneering research in musical acoustics, particularly on tanpura. He worked out the theory of transverse vibration of bowed strings, on the basis of superposition velocities.

He was also the first to investigate the harmonic nature of the sound of the Indian drums such as the tabla and the mridangam.

He died on 21 November 1970 at Bangalore.

India celebrates National Science Day on 28 February of every year to commemorate the discovery of the Raman Effect in 1928.

❖❖❖

84

Srinivasa Ramanujan

(1887-1920)

Srinivasa Ramanujan Iyengar was an Indian mathematician who made substantial contributions to mathematical analysis, number theory, infinite series and continued fractions. He is best known for his work on hypergeometric series and continued fractions.

Srinivasa Ramanujan was born at Erode, India, on December 22, 1887.

He attended school in nearby Kumbakonam. By the time he was 13, he could solve unaided every problem in *Loney's Trigonometry,* and at 14 he obtained the theorems for the sine and the cosine that had been anticipated by L. Euler.

In 1903 he came upon George Shoobridge Carr's *Synopsis of Elementary Results in Pure and Applied Mathematics.* The book opened a whole new world to him, and he set out to establish the 6,165 theorems in it for himself. Having no contact with good books, he had to do original research for each solution. Trying to devise his own methods, he made some astounding discoveries, among them several new algebraic series.

Ramanujan became so absorbed in mathematics that when he entered the local government college in 1904 with a merit scholarship, he neglected his other subjects and lost the scholarship. Despite two later attempts, he never qualified for the first degree in arts. While working as a clerk he continued his mathematical investigations; in 1911 he started to publish some of his results.

In January 1913 Ramanujan sent some of his work to G.H. Hardy, lecturer in mathematics at Cambridge. Hardy noticed that whereas Ramanujan had rediscovered, and gone far beyond, some of the latest conclusions of Western mathematicians, he was completely ignorant of some of the most fundamental areas. In May the University of Madras gave Ramanujan a scholarship.

In 1914 Ramanujan went to Cambridge. In Hardy's opinion, if Ramanujan's gift had been recognised early, he could have become one of the greatest mathematicians of all time. In hypergeometric series and continued fractions, "he was unquestionably one of the great masters." Ramanujan had an intimate familiarity with numbers, and excelled especially in number theory and modular function theory. His patience, memory, power of calculation, and intuition made him the greatest formalist of his day.

Ramanujan was awarded in 1916 the B.A. Degree by research of the Cambridge University. In 1918 he was elected a fellow of the Royal Society and a Fellow of Trinity College, Cambridge.

Ramanujan published some of his results in journals, and many are beautiful indeed. However, his working notebooks contained much additional unorganised material which remained uninvestigated until the sustained efforts of Berndt and his coworkers who systematically examined and proved Ramanujan's sometimes vague or ambiguous statements.

He died on April 26, 1920.

The *Collected Papers of Ramanujan* was edited by Profs. G.H.Hardy, P.V. Seshu Aiyar and B.M. Wilson and first published by Cambridge University Press in 1927 (later by Chelsea, 1962; and by Narosa, 1987), seven years after his death. His 'Lost' Notebook was found in the estate of Prof. G.N. Watson in the spring of 1976 by Prof. George Andrews of Pennsylvania State University, and its facsimile edition was brought out by Narosa Publishing House in 1987, on the occasion of Ramanujan's birth centenary. His original *Note Books* have been edited in a series of five volumes by Bruce C. Berndt (*Ramanujan Note Books*, Springer, Parts I to V, 1985 onwards).

His bust was commissioned by Professors R. Askey, S. Chandrasekhar, G.E. Andrews, Bruce C. Berndt, and more than one hundred mathematicians and scientists contributed money for the bust sculpted by Paul Granlund in 1984; another was commissioned for the Ramanujan Institute of the University of Madras, by Mr. Masilamani in 1994.

❖❖❖

85

Satyajit Ray

(1921-1992)

Satyajit Ray is perhaps the most well known Indian filmmaker to the Western World and inarguably among the dozen or so great masters of world cinema. He made his films in Bengali, yet, his films are of universal interest. He won an Oscar for lifetime achievement in films and the Bharat Ratna award in 1992.

Satyajit Ray was born on May 2, 1921 in Calcutta.

As a youngster, Ray developed significant interest in music, especially Western Classical music. He graduated from the Ballygunge Government School and studied Economics at Presidency College.

In 1940, he studied art at Kala Bhavan, Rabindranath Tagore's University in Shantiniketan, West Bengal. He learned to draw from the great master-teacher Nandalal Bose, a pioneer in art education in Modern India.

Without completing the five-year course, he returned to Calcutta in 1943, to join the British-owned advertising agency D. J. Keymer as a visualiser. Within a few years, he rose to be its art director. In 1947 he established the Calcutta Film Society.

In 1950, he was asked by a major Calcutta publisher to illustrate a children's edition of *Pather Panchali*, Bibhuti Bhushan Banerjee's semi-autobiographical novel. Ray ended up sketching the entire book. These formed the kernel and the essential visual elements in the making of *Pather Panchali*, Ray's very first film and the film that brought him instant international recognition and fame. At the Cannes Film Festival, in 1956, Ray received in absentia, the Best Human Document Award for this hauntingly beautiful film.

Ray was now a full-time professional filmmaker. A prolific filmmaker, during his lifetime Ray directed 36 films, comprising features, documentaries and short stories. These include the renowned Apu trilogy (*Pather Panchali, Aparajito* (1956) and *Apur Sansar* (1959)), *Jalsaghar* (1958), *Postmaster (*1961), *Charulata* (1964), *Days and Nights in the Forest* (1969) and *Pikoo* (1980) along with a host of his lesser known works which themselves stand up as fine examples of story telling. His films encompass a diversity of moods, techniques, and genres: comedy, satire, fantasy and tragedy. Usually he made films in a realist mode, but he also experimented with surrealism and fantasy.

The inner struggle between traditional and modern values in Indian life has coloured several other Ray films. *Devi* (The Goddess, 1960) is essentially a story exploring the dangers of religious fanaticism and superstition. To mark the centenary of the birth of Rabindranath Tagore, Ray made *Teen Kanya* (Three Daughters) in 1961.

Ray's first original script was for Kanchanjungha (1962), which was also his first picture in colour and the first film for which Ray composed the score. Yet another disillusioned character is the taxi-driver protagonist of *Abhijan* (The Expedition, 1962). In *Mahanagar* (The Big City, 1963), Ray tackles the problem of whether or not both a husband and wife should take up jobs to maintain the family. The Big City is set in contemporary India, but the issue at stake - that being a woman's place in society - is essentially the same in *Charulata* (1964), which takes place in 1879 and is based on another story by Tagore. Films such as *Kapurush-o-Mahapurush* (The Crowd and the Holy Man, 1965), *Nayak*

(The Hero, 1966) and *Chiriakhana* (The Zoo, 1967) contain little of Ray's personal touch. It was not until *Aranyer Din Ratri* (Days and Nights in the Forest, 1969) that Ray returned to form.

During the late 1960s, Ray made a fairytale for adults in *Goopy Gyn Bagha Byne* (The Adventures of Goopy and Bagha, 1968) and then went on to make The City Trilogy, comprising *Pratidwandi* (The Adversary, 1970), *Seemabaddha* (Company Limited, 1971) and *Jana Aranya* (The Middleman, 1975). Two documentaries from this period are Sikkim (1971), and *The Inner Eye* (1972), a short tribute to the blind artist Binod Behari Mukherjee. Between these two documentaries, however, Ray made *Ashani Sanket* (Distant Thunder, 1973), and his second colour film, *Shatranji Ke Kilharia* period piece set in Lucknow 1856.

Ray returned to making films for children, such as *Joi Baba Felunath* (The Elephant God, 1978) and *Hirok Rajar Deshe* (The Kingdom of Diamonds, 1980), a sequel to *Goopy and Bagha*.

His last writing, *My Years With Apu*, was published posthumously in 1994. He wrote some seventy novellas, stories and translations and each one of them became a best seller in Bengali.

In 1981, Ray was commissioned to make a film for Indian TV. The resulting film was *Sadgati* (Deliverance) a 50-minute piece filmed in Hindi, which relates a story of callous exploitation.

In 1984 Ray made *Ghare-Baire* (The Home and the World). Due to a heart attack in 1983, he was told by his doctors not to do any location work and he was forced to shoot in studios. Unfortunately, this constraint of shooting does mar the last of his films: *Ganashatru* (Enemy of the People, 1989), *Shakha Prashakha* (Branches of the Tree, 1990) and *Agantuk* (The Stranger, 1991),

In 1992, Satyajit Ray was honoured with an Oscar for Lifetime Achievement. He received the award from his sickbed in Calcutta, through a special live satellite-television event.

The award was followed by the Indian Government's recognition in the form of the Bharat Ratna, the ultimate honour for any Indian.

He died on April 23, 1992 in Calcutta.

❖❖❖

86

Rembrandt

(1606-1669)

Rembrandt Harmenszoon van Rijn was a Dutch painter and etcher. He is best known for his expressive use of chiaroscuro in his many portraits. His name still symbolises a whole period of art history rightfully known as 'Holland's Golden Age'.

Rembrandt was born in Leiden on July 15, 1606.

For seven years Rembrandt was a student at the Latin school, and then, in 1620, he enrolled at the university. After only a few months, however, he left to become a painter. He was an apprentice of the painter Jacob Isaacsz van Swanenburgh for three years.

In 1624 Rembrandt went to Amsterdam to work with Pieter Lastman, a painter of biblical, mythological, and historical scenes. It was not long before he was a master at his craft. At 22 he began taking on students of his own.

The earliest works by Rembrandt, beginning with the *Stoning of St. Stephen* (1625), show some imitation of Lastman's style, applied to scenes in which a number of figures are involved in a dramatic action.

By 1625 Rembrandt was working independently in Leiden. In addition to his narrative subjects, Rembrandt was practising with pen, brush, and etcher's needle the depiction of emotions conveyed by facial expressions. Throughout his career he was his own most frequent model, wearing gold chains and plumed hats, testing his skill at depicting varied textures.

By 1631 wealthy patrons commissioned portraits. *The Portrait of Nicolaes Ruts* is an example of the type of portraits he painted during that period. A major commission soon came to him: *Dr. Nicolaas Tulp Demonstrating the Anatomy of the Arm* (1632). For this large canvas Rembrandt devised a new unified composition for the traditional "anatomy lesson".

In 1631 Rembrandt moved to Amsterdam, where his career and his personal life prospered. Besides painting portraits his mythological and religious works were much in demand. Works of art such as *The Blinding of Samson* and *Stormy Landscape* had people in awe of his vision.

Rembrandt's works of the middle 1630s were his most baroque. This is most explicit in the scenes from the *Passion of Christ* (1633-1639) and *Angel Appearing to the Shepherds* (1634). Landscape paintings also emerged, such as the *Landscape with an Obelisk*. *The Visitation* (1640) serves well to sum up Rembrandt's style at this transitional point in his development. The famous *Night Watch* (1642) may be considered as one of his last truly baroque works.

About 1640 Rembrandt developed a new interest in landscape which persisted through the next two decades. The etched *View of Amsterdam* (ca. 1640) and *Winter Landscape* (1646) has all the earmarks of having been painted from life, on the spot.

In contrast with Rembrandt's dramatic religious compositions of the earlier period, those of the 1640s tend to be quiet, with exquisitely controlled light casting an almost palpable spiritual glow on scenes that might otherwise seem to depict humble everyday life. Examples are *Holy Family* (1646) and *Hundred Guilder Print*.

In 1652 a Sicilian nobleman commissioned a painting from Rembrandt: *Aristotle Contemplating a Bust of Homer*. The lavish impasto, the scintillating white and gold contrasted with velvety blacks, and the quality of inwardness and self-communion are characteristic features of Rembrandt's style at this time. Another important commission for a group portrait came to Rembrandt in 1656: the *Anatomy Lesson of Dr. Joan Deyman.*

During these times some of his greatest works were created. *The Jewish Bride, The Syndics of the Cloth Guild, Bathsheba, Jacob Blessing the Sons of Joseph,* and a *Self Portrait* (1669) saw much success. In his last years Rembrandt produces several masterpieces, such as *David and Saul* (1657) and *The Jewish Bride* (1665). In 1658 he painted the small and sensitive *Jupiter and Mercury Visiting Philemon and Baucis,* which was based on a painting by Adam Elsheimer.

In 1660-1661 Rembrandt painted an enormous canvas commissioned for the splendid new town hall in Amsterdam. It was the *Conspiracy of the Batavians,* or the *Oath of Julius.* The scene of the oath was painted broadly, to be viewed from a distance, and in the most luminous colours. In 1662 he painted the *Sampling Officials of the Drapers' Guild.* The beautiful pair of late portraits, *Man with a Magnifying Glass* and *Lady with a Pink,* have few peers in all the realm of art.

When he died, on October 4, 1669, a painting, *Simeon with the Christ Child in the Temple,* was left unfinished on his easel.

❖❖❖

87

Arundhati Roy

(1961-)

Suzanna Arundhati Roy is an Indian writer and activist who won the Booker Prize in 1997 for her novel, 'The God of Small Things', the 2002 Lannan Cultural Freedom Prize and the Sydney Peace Prize in 2004.

Arundhati Roy was born November 24, 1961 in Assam.

At the age of 16 Arundhati enrolled at the Delhi School of Architecture. This training, like her elementary education, proved instrumental in shaping her as a writer. In *The Salon Interview,* she likens the creation of a piece of literature to that of plans for a building. There she met her first husband, Gerard Da Cunha, a fellow architecture student. Their marriage lasted four years. She quit the course as she did not have great love for architecture.

She took a job at the National Institute of Urban Affairs, Delhi. One day film director Pradeep Krishen saw her cycling down a street and offered her a small role of tribal girl in the film *Massey Saab.* She accepted the role after initial reservations. She later married him.

Meanwhile, she got a scholarship to go to Italy for eight months to study the restoration of monuments.

After returning from Italy Arundhati wrote screenplays for a couple of TV films, *In Which Annie Gives It Those Ones* and *Electric Moon.* She then published a criticism of the acclaimed film,

Shekhar Kapur's *Bandit Queen*; the controversy that followed resulted in a lawsuit against her.

Roy retired to private life focusing her energies on *The God of Small Things*, which was published in April 1997. About six months later it was awarded the Booker Prize; Roy is the first Indian woman ever to achieve this honor. The book has been a stunning success both in India, and internationally. This novel proved to be a success as it was published in 19 countries and 16 languages. She was compared to Charles Dickens and William Faulkner for the way she deals with the issues of race, class, and society.

The acclaim that Roy garnered made her an instant celebrity, but the traditional trappings of literary fame were accompanied by a certain amount of notoriety due to the book's controversial treatment of delicate subject matter. Charges of anti-Communism were leveled against Roy because of her portrayal of the Communist characters. In addition, Roy faced charges of obscenity and demands that the final chapter of the book be removed because of its sexual content.

After winning the Booker Prize for *The God of Small Things*, Arundhati Roy has put her talents and status to use as an activist for several of the important issues facing India today. She has spoken out against the oppression of the Dalits and appeared at a reception in Kerala to publicly declare herself an advocate of their cause. She also contributed materially, by donating the royalties from the Malayalam translation of *The God of Small Things* to advance Dalit literary efforts and help Dalit writers to tell their stories to the world.

Most recently, Roy has been involved in protesting against the Narmada Dam Project. Her article "The Greater Common Good" in *Frontline* disparages a project that could force millions to abandon their homes in order to provide limited benefits to a limited number of people. She has demonstrated against construction of the dam both in the Narmada Valley, and globally in an effort to heighten awareness and obtain support for the cause.

She has written on varied topics such as Narmada Dam project, India's nuclear weapons and American power giant Enron's activities in India.

Arundhati Roy is strongly associated with anti-globalisation movement and is a staunch critic of neo-imperialism.

❖❖❖

88

Michael Schumacher

(1969-)

Michael Schumacher is a former German Formula One driver, seven-time world champion, and current advisor and occasional test driver for Ferrari.

Michael Schumacher was born on January 3, 1969, near Cologne, Germany.

As a four-year old Michael enjoyed playing on a pedal kart, though when his father fitted it with a small motorcycle engine the future superstar promptly crashed into a lamppost. But he quickly mastered his machine and won his first kart championship at six, following which his parents arranged sponsorship from wealthy enthusiasts that enabled Michael to make rapid progress.

By 1987 he was German and European kart champion and had left school to work as an apprentice car mechanic, a job that was soon replaced by full-time employment as a race driver.

In 1990 he won the German Formula Three championship and was hired by Mercedes to drive sports cars. By 1991 he was racing Formula One cars. He made a stunning Formula One debut, qualifying an astonishing seventh in a Jordan for the Belgian Grand Prix at Spa, whereupon he was immediately snapped up by Benetton. He won his first Grand Prix a year later.

In 1992 he won his first Formula One race, again at Spa, the most demanding circuit of them all.

Over the next four seasons with Benetton he won a further 18 races and two world championships. His first, in 1994, was somewhat tainted in that Benetton was suspected of technical irregularities and in their championship showdown race in Adelaide Schumacher collided (deliberately, some thought) with his closest challenger, the Williams of Damon Hill. But Germany's first world champion was unquestionably worthy of the 1995 driving title.

Following this he moved to Ferrari, then a team in disarray and without a champion since Jody Scheckter in 1979. The Schumacher-Ferrari combination began promisingly with three wins in 1996 and five more in 1997, though that season ended in humiliation when in the final race, at Jerez in Spain, Schumacher tried unsuccessfully to ram the Williams of his title rival Jacques Villeneuve off the road. As punishment Schumacher's points and his second place in the championship were stricken from the record books he would thereafter begin to rewrite.

After finishing second overall in 1998, Schumacher's 1999 season was interrupted by a crash at Silverstone where he received a broken leg that kept him out of action for several races. From then on there was no stopping 'Schumi', who in 2000 became Ferrari's first champion in 21 years, then went on to win the driving title for the next four years in succession. In 2002 he won 11 of the 17 races and finished on the podium in all of them.

His 2004 year is now legendary: he won 13 of the 18 races, extending his career total to 83 and claimed an unprecedented seventh overall championship. He remained a dominant force in the sport of Formula 1 racing through 2006, when he retired at the end of the season. His final race was the Brazilian Grand Prix on 22 October 2006.

In March 2007, Michael had a corner named in his honour at the Nurburgring, the venue for the 2007 German Grand Prix. The fast left-right switchback after the Dunlop hairpin was renamed the 'Schumacher S' in deference to the seven-time world champion, who retired thereafter.

In April 2007, Michael honoured the success of his country in the A1GP World Cup of Motorsport, presenting A1 Team Germany with the World Cup trophy at the series' end of season awards ceremony. He received a standing ovation from the gathered crowd when he was announced on stage.

In September 2007 Michael was named the official 'Global Social Responsibility Ambassador' for Bacardi. In the same month and year Michael was awarded one of Spain's highest honours, the Prince of Asturias prize for sports.

Rich beyond his wildest dreams, he generously uses his fortune to help those less fortunate. He supports charities, especially those for underprivileged children. He gave 1.15 million euros ($2.5 million) to UNESCO in 2005, and $US10 million ($12 million) a year later to help the victims of the earthquake and tsunami in Southeast Asia.

❖❖❖

89

Shankaracharya

(686-718)

One of the greatest philosophers of India, Adi Shankaracharya founded the Advaita Vedanta, which is based on the concept of non duality. He had a profound influence on the growth of Hinduism through his non-dualistic philosophy. He advocated the greatness and importance of the important Hindu scriptures, the Vedas, and gave new life to Hinduism at a time when Buddhism and Jainism were gaining popularity.

Adi Shankaracharya was born around the year 686 in the village of Kaladi in Kerala, India.

At the age of eight, Shankara had mastered all four *Vedas* and six *Shastras*. By the time he was 12 years of age, he had understood all branches of knowledge. And by 16 he had written commentaries on those *Vedantas* which are considered to be his major works.

Even at a young age Shankara had become proficient in Prakrit Magadhi and Sanskrit languages.

He was sent to the nearby Gurukula on the banks of river Poornaa. Under the guidance of Guru he studied the *Vedas* and its branches and also all other subjects.

He realised that Monism/Advaita was the essence of all knowledge. He took his mother's permission to renounce worldly life so that he could teach his ideas to the world.

He was the founder of the Dasnami Sanyasa Tradition (a tradition of ascetics). He consolidated the various schools of worship and brought them under the Advaita Philosophy principle. He propounded the Vedantic tenet that Brahman the Supreme and man are of one essence and that all people should strive to cultivate this vision of oneness.

He established four spiritual centres in the four corners of the country, thus upholding the underlying unity of the holy land of Bharat. The four centres are at Sringeri, Karnataka in the south, Joshimath, Uttarakhand in the north, Puri, Orissa in the east, and Dwaraka, Gujarat in the west. For each centre, he gave responsibility to one of his disciples

The *Upanishads, Bhagavad Gita* and *Brahma Sutras* are sacred scriptures of the Hindus; but it is not easy to understand them. Shankaracharya wrote commentaries on the *Upanishads* and the *Bhagavad Gita*. They became very popular.

Shankaracharya went to Badrinath in the Himalayas to write his commentary on the *Brahma Sutras*. Dedicating himself to the service of Ishwara and Bhagavan Vyasa, he launched upon his work.

Now Shankara's main aim was to search for a Guru. He came to the banks of river where he found the hermitage of a Mahayogi, Govinda Bhagavatpada. After prostrating before the Guru, he requested that he may be accepted as a disciple. Govinda Yogi felt happy at the very first meeting as he had found the very type of person - the fittest disciple – for whom he had been waiting. Taking initiation from the Guru in a regular way to ascetic life, Shankara carried on his studies with all devotion. Under his guidance, Shankara mastered everything in *Hatha, Raja* and *Jnana Yoga* in only three years, after which he received initiation in the knowledge of Brahma. The entire world appeared to be full of Brahman to him. After this the only thing that remained to be done was to communicate the bliss he had known and experienced to one and all through Vedanta.

According to Swami Satyeswarandana Giri in his biography series *Babaji,* Vol 1, 'The Divine Himalayan Yogi', Shankaracharya was also blessed by the Ageless Yogi, Maha Muni Babaji, who taught him perfection of the *Raja Yoga* disciplines. He practised in the Himalayas at Kedarnath how to attain the spontaneous state of consciousness.

Shankara's new knowledge of the secrets of *Dharana, Dhyana* and *Samadhi* expanded his spiritual powers and accomplishments.

Shankaracharya has written around 50 texts, most of them being hymns, and commentaries on spiritual texts like the Vedas and Upanishads. Some of them are *Saundarya Lahari, Shivananda Lahari,* and the famous *Bhaja Govindam* that extols devotion. He also wrote of attachment in the *Moha Mudgara.*

Adi Shankaracharya lived for just 32 years, but could create an unparalleled legacy.

❖❖❖

90

George Bernard Shaw

(1856–1950)

George Bernard Shaw was an Anglo-Irish playwright, critic, pamphleteer and amateur photographer. He was awarded the 1925 Nobel Prize for literature.

Shaw was born in Dublin, Ireland, on July 16, 1856.

At an early age he was tutored in classics by an uncle, and studied at the Wesleyan Connexional School in Dublin. He studied music and art at the same time.

He became a Dublin office boy in 1871. He then joined his mother and two sisters in London, where they conducted a music school.

Shaw had started writing, at the age of 16, criticism and reviews for Irish newspapers and magazines. He also entertained in London society as a singer.

In 1876 he wrote his first music criticisms for *The Hornet.* He became music critic of *The Star* in 1888-9; in 1890 he transferred to *The World* and continued to write weekly criticism until August 1894, but by then had already begun writing essays, political pamphlets, books and plays.

Between 1876 and 1885 Shaw wrote five novels. *Immaturity,* the first, remained unpublished, and the other four, after a series of rejections from London publishers, appeared in radical periodicals. To-Day published his *An Unsocial Socialist* in 1884.

The Irrational Knot, a portrayal of modern marriage that Shaw asserted anticipated Henrik Ibsen's *A Doll's House,* appeared in another radical periodical, *Our Corner,* as did *Love among the Artists* (1887-1888).

Shaw joined the Fabian Society in 1884. *Fabian Essays* (1887), edited by Shaw, emphasized the importance of economics and class structure; for him, economics was "the basis of society". For 27 years he served on the Fabian Society's executive committee. He published *Common Sense about the War* in 1914, a criticism of the British government and its policies. *The Intelligent Woman's Guide to Capitalism and Socialism* (1928) supplied a complete summary of his political position. It remains a major volume of socialist commentary.

Between 1888 and 1894 he wrote for newspapers and periodicals as a highly successful music critic. He began writing on a regular basis for Frank Harris's *Saturday Review.* His *Quintessence of Ibsenism* appeared in 1890, *The Sanity of Art* in 1895, and *The Perfect Wagnerite* in 1898.

Shaw wrote drama between 1892 and 1947, when he completed *Buoyant Billions* at the age of 91. *Widowers' Houses,* his first play, was produced in 1892 at London's Royalty Theatre. He wrote *The Philanderers* and *Mrs. Warren's Profession* in 1893.

Shaw's first stage successes, *Arms and the Man* and *Candida,* were produced in 1894. *You Never Can Tell,* first produced in 1896, is Shaw's most underrated comedy.

Shaw's miraculous period began with *Man and Superman* (1901-1903). It was miraculous even for him; in a late play, *Too True to Be Good* (1932. *Major Barbara* (1905) is a drama of ideas, largely about poverty and capitalism. *Androcles and the Lion* (1911) discusses religion. *John Bull's Other Island* (1904concerns political relations between England and Ireland. *Heartbreak House* (between 1913 and 1916)analyses the domestic effects of World War I. Most of the plays after *Arms and the Man* carry long prefaces that are often not directly related to the drama itself. Shaw systematically explored such topics as marriage, parenthood, education and poverty in the prefaces.

Heartbreak House, Back to Methuselah (1921, *Androcles and the Lion, Pygmalion* (1914) and *Saint Joan* (1923) are considered his best plays. *Pygmalion* was adapted 50 years later into the Broadway musical *My Fair Lady.* Shaw also won an Oscar in 1938 for his screenplay for a non-musical movie version of *Pygmalion.*

Shaw won the 1925 Nobel Prize for Literature. He remains the only person to win both an Oscar and a Nobel Prize.

Shaw died in England, on November 2, 1950.

❖❖❖

91

M.S. Subbulakshmi

(1916-2004)

Madurai Shanmukhavadivu Subbulakshmi, popularly known as M.S., was a renowned Indian Carnatic vocalist. She was the first musician ever to be awarded the Bharat Ratna. Also known as the Nightingale of India, she was also the recipient of Padma Bhushan, Padma Vibhushan and Ramon Magsaysay Award.

Subbulakshmi was born as Kunjamma into a family of musicians in Madurai, on September 16, 1916.

Subbulakshmi (M.S.) started learning Carnatic music from a very early age. She began training under Semmangudi Srinivasa Iyer and then under Pandit Narayan Rao Vyas.

She made her debut as a singer at the age of eight and went on to perform in concerts. She released her first album at the mere age of 10. She gave her first public performance at Kumbakonam during Mahamaham festival.

By the age of 17, M.S. was giving major performances at the Madras Music Academy, the prestigious centre for the study and promotion of Carnatic music. Since then, she performed countless musical forms in different languages such as Hindi, Bengali, Gujarati, Tamil, Malayalam, Telugu, Sanskrit and Kannada.

In 1940, she married T. Sadasivam, a freedom fighter, and a follower of Rajaji. He played a key role in advancing her career.

M.S. became famous as a film actress. Her first movie *Sevasadanam* was released in 1938. She also played the male role of Narada in *Savitri* (1941) to raise money for launching *Kalki*, her husband's nationalist Tamil weekly. Her most memorable role was of the Rajasthani saint-poetess Meera in the eponymous film (1945), re-made in Hindi in 1947, for which she sang the famous Meera bhajans. These renditions continue to haunt listeners to this day. She quit films and turned wholly to concert music.

M.S. travelled to London, New York, Canada, the Far East, and other places as India's cultural ambassador. Her concerts at Carnegie Hall, New York; the UN General Assembly on UN day in 1966 (while U Thant was the Secretary General); the Royal Albert Hall, London in 1982; and at the Festival of India in Moscow in 1987 were significant landmarks in her career. She was applauded by not just Indians, but foreigners as well.

Mahatma Gandhi was so charmed of her Meera bhajans that he requested her to sing the song *Hari Tum haro Jan ki bheer* (Lord, please dispel the fear in mankind). She regretfully declined as she had a cold that day. A prompt reply came back from the Mahatma's side saying "I would gladly hear Subbulakshmi speak it than hear it sung by others."

In the late 1950s, as she sang at the Ramakrishna Ashram in Delhi, Prime Minister Jawaharlal Nehruwas among the audience. At the end of the recital he was so moved that he bowed, and said, "What am I, a mere prime minister, before a queen of music!"

Some of her most famous works include *Suprabhatam, Bhajagovindam, Kurai Onrum Illai, Vishnu Sahasranamam, Hanuman Chalisa, Vaishnava Janato*, etc.

She was widely honoured, praised and awarded: Padma Bhushan in 1954, Sangeetha Kalanidhi in 1968, Ramon Magsaysay award in 1974, Padma Vibhushan in 1975, Kalidasa Samman in 1988, Indira Gandhi Award for National Integration in 1990, and Bharat Ratna in 1998. She was also honoured as the court-singer of Tirumala Tirupati Devasthanams.

She rendered Kanchi Mahaswamigal's composition *Maithreem Bhajatha* in her concert at the UN in 1966. She donated many of the royalties on several best sold records to many charity organisations.

With the death of her husband Sadhasivam in 1997, she stopped all her public performances.

M.S. passed away on December 11, 2004 after a brief illness.

❖❖❖

92

Rabindranath Tagore

(1861-1941)

Rabindranath Tagore was a Bengali poet, novelist, visual artist, playwright, composer and educator, who won the Nobel Prize for Literature in 1913. He was knighted in 1915, but he surrendered it in 1919 as a protest against the massacre in Jallianwala Bagh.

Rabindranath Tagore was born on 7 May 1861 in Calcutta.

He was first admitted into Oriental Seminary School, but failing to flourish in the conventional school system, he studied, with tutors at home, art, history, science, mathematics, Bengali, Sanskrit, English, *Upanishads*, Romantic poetry like that of Percy Bysshe Shelley and classical poetry, notably that of Kalidasa. Later he went to Bengal Academy and St Xaviers School for brief periods.

In 1874, his first published poem *Abhilaash* (Desire) was published anonymously in a magazine called *Tattobodhini*. In 1875, for the first time, a poem with credit to his name was published in *Amrita Bazar Patrika* (weekly). He translated *Macbeth* into Bengali verse which was later published in *Bharati* magazine. Following the style of Vaisnava Padalvali (verses), he wrote *Bhanusingher Padavali* under the penname of Bhanusingha.

He was influenced in his writings by his elder brother Jyotirindranath and his wife Kadambari Devi. Two magazines,

Bharati and *Balaka* were published from the Tagore house and he regularly contributed to those.

He also started writing short stories including his first *Bhikharini* (The Beggar Woman, 1877). His first book of poems, *Kabi Kahini* (The Tale of a Poet) was published in 1878. Then, with the intent to become a barrister, he was off to England to attend the University College in London from 1878-1880, although he did not finish his degree. Retuning to India in 1880, he wrote two musical plays: *Valmiki Prativa* (The Genius of Valmiki) and *Kalmrigaya* (The Fatal Hunt) – and acted in these plays too. He wrote *Sandhya Sangeet* (Evening Songs) and *Nirjharer Swapnabhanga* (The Fountain Awakened from its Dream) (1882). In 1884 he wrote a collection of poems, *Kori-o-kamal* (Sharp and Flats). In 1886 he wrote the musical drama, *Mayar Khela, Raja-o-rani* (King and Queen) and *Visarjan* (Sacrifice).

In 1890 Tagore moved to the vast family estate in Shilaidaha, a region now part of Bangladesh. He gained much inspiration from the people and the landscape and it became a prolific period of writing for him, works including *Chitra: A Play in One Act* (1896), *Manasi* (The Ideal One — poetry, 1890), *Sonar Tari* (The Golden Boat — poetry, 1894), and the famous dance/musical drama, *Chitrangada*. In 1894 he wrote the famous collection of poems, *Sonar Tari* (The Golden Boat).

In 1901 he took the editorial charge of the magazine *Bangadarshan*. He established the Bolpur Bramhacharya ashram at Shantiniketan, a school in the pattern of old Indian Ashrama.

When Tagore's wife died in 1902 he composed *Smaran* (In Memoriam), a collection of poems, dedicated to his wife.

Other works written or published during this period were *Katha O Kahini* (Tales and Stories, 1900), *Naivedya* (Offering — poetry, 1901), *Kheya* (poetry, 1906), *Raja* (play, 1910), *Dak-ghar*

(The Post Office, 1912), *The Crescent Moon* (1913), *Gitimalya* (Wreath of Songs, 1914), *Songs of Kabir* (1915), *Stray Birds* (1916), *Sadhana: The Realisation of Life* (1916), and *Balaka* (The Flight of Cranes, 1916), and the poems *Fruit-Gathering* (1916), *The Fugitive* (1921) and *The Gardener* (1915).

He strongly protested against Lord Curzon's decision to divide Bengal on the basis of religion. He wrote a number of national songs and attended protest meetings. He introduced the Rakhibandhan ceremony, symbolising the underlying unity in undivided Bengal.

In 1909 he started writing *Gitanjali* (Song Offerings) from Silaidaha. First published in 1910, *Gitanjali* was translated to English in 1912. It includes an Introduction by W. B.Yeats, and Rothenstein did a pencil sketch for the cover page. The book created a sensation in English literary world.

As a patriot, he composed the music and lyrics for India's national anthem *Jana-Gana-Mana* in 1911 and when Bangladesh became independent in 1971 they chose his song *Amar Sonar Bangla* as its national anthem.

Ezra Pound's *Poetry Magazine* published Tagore's six *Gitanjali* poems in its December 1912 issue.

On 26 December, 1913, the University of Calcutta conferred on him the honorary degree of "D.Litt". In 1915 he was bestowed a knighthood by the British Crown, though he renounced it in 1919 due to the Jallianwala Bagh Massacre. It was one of many political statements Tagore made during his lifetime.

In 1921, he established the Viswabharati University. He gave all his money from Nobel Prize and royalty money from his books to this University. In the same year Tagore and agricultural economist Leonard Elmhirst founded the Institute for Rural Reconstruction, "Shriniketan" near Santiniketan.

He went to South America where he met Argentine poet Madam Victoria Ocampo at Buenos Ayres. The poet wrote *Purabi,* a collection of poems dedicated to her.

In 1940 Oxford University arranged a special ceremony in Santiniketan to honour the poet with Doctorate of Literature.

The famous polymath is fondly remembered and esteemed for his hundreds of poems and songs popularly known as Rabindrasangeet; his vast collection of paintings and drawings; and the various dramas, novels, essays, operas, short stories, travel diaries, correspondence, and autobiographies that he wrote.

Tagore passed away on 7 August, 1941 in his ancestral home in Calcutta.

93

J.R.D. Tata

(1904-1993)

Jehangir Ratanji Dadabhoy Tata was a pioneer aviator and an important businessman of India. He was India's first pilot. He launched Air India International as India's first international airline. He won the Bharat Ratna in 1992.

Jehangir Ratanji Dadabhoy Tata was born in Paris on July 29, 1904.

JRD Tata was educated in France, Japan and England before being drafted into the French army for a mandatory one-year period. He joined Tata & Sons as an unpaid apprentice in 1925.

On February 10, 1929, JRD became the first Indian to pass the pilot's examination and to become India's first pilot. He was instrumental in building Tata Airlines, which ultimately became Air India. His passion for flying was fulfilled with the formation of the Tata Aviation Service in 1932.

In 1938, he was elected Chairman of Tata & Sons, making him the head of the largest industrial group in India. He started with 14 enterprises under his leadership and half a century later on July 26, 1988, when he left, Tata & Sons was a conglomerate of 95 enterprises.

JRD was the trustee of Sir Dorabji Tata Trust from its inception in 1932. Under his guidance, this Trust established Asia's first cancer hospital, the Tata Memorial Centre for Cancer, Research and Treatment, Bombay, in 1941. He also founded the Tata Institute of Social Sciences, 1936 (TISS), the Tata Institute of Fundamental

Research, 1945 (TIFR), and the National Centre for Performing Arts.

Just before India's Independence, Tata Steel promoted the Tata Engineering and Locomotive Company (TELCO) in 1945 with an objective to produce locomotives for the Indian Railways. Today it has emerged as the country's largest Commercial Vehicle producer.

In 1948, JRD launched Air India International as India's first international airline. In 1953, the Indian Government appointed him as Chairman of Air India and a director on the Board of Indian Airlines. He was bestowed with the title of Honorary Air Commodore of India.

In 1956, JRD initiated a programme of closer "employee association with management" to give workers a stronger voice in the affairs of the company. He espoused the principles of an eight-hour working day, free medical aid, workers' provident scheme, and workmen's accident compensation schemes, which were later adopted as statutory requirements in India.

JRD's Tata Consultancy Service (TCS) has developed a computer system to expedite the spread of literacy all over India.

JRD received a number of awards: Padma Vibhushan in 1957, Guggenheim Medal for aviation in 1988, Bharat Ratna in 1992. In the same year, he was also bestowed with the United Nations Population Award for his crusading endeavours towards initiating and successfully implementing the family planning movement in India, much before it became an official government policy.

JRD Tata died in Geneva, Switzerland on November 29, 1993 at the age of 89.

❖❖❖

94

Tim Berners–Lee

(1955-)

Sir Timothy John Berners-Lee is the primary inventor of the World Wide Web. In 2003, Queen Elizabeth II mad him a Knight Commander of the Order of the British Empire (KBE) for his work on the Web. In 2004, he was awarded the first Millennium Technology Prize, a Finland-based award for excellence which carries a cash prize of one million Euros.

Timothy John Berners-Lee was born on 8 June 1955 in London, England.

By the time he enrolled at Queens College, Oxford in 1973, Berners-Lee was a keen inventor and built his first computer there with such makeshift materials. He and a friend were caught hacking and banned from using the university computer.

After graduating in 1976, Berners-Lee worked for the telecommunications equipment manufacturer Plessey Telecommunications at Poole in Dorset and then worked for various companies as a freelance software engineer.

He set about developing a software programme by enabling computers to make – and to store – random associations between disparate pieces of information. He wrote the first such programme, Enquire (Enquire-Within-Upon-Everything) in 1980 while working at CERN, the European Particle Physics Laboratory in Geneva. Intended only for his private use, he never published Enquire, but continued to develop similar programmes throughout the 1980s. He first described the concept of a global system, based on the concept of 'hypertext', that would allow researchers anywhere to share information. He worked on ways of combining the internet and hypertext.

In 1989, he published a paper called 'Information Management: A Proposal' in which he combine hypertext with the Internet, to create a system for sharing and distributing information not just within a company, but globally. He named it the *World Wide Web.* By the end of 1990 he circulated his work on the World Wide Web within CERN and then made it more widely available, together with the first web server, named *httpd,* in the research and scientific communities.

He also created the first web browser and editor. The world's first website, *http://info.cern.ch,* was launched on 6 August 1991. It explained the World Wide Web concept and gave users an introduction to getting started with their own websites. He went on to ensure that his invention would be freely accessible to everyone and to eradicate the risk of the web being controlled by commercial forces. From the beginning, he waived his right to patent his design or to earn royalties from its use thereby establishing the web as a non-commercial medium.

In 1994, Berners-Lee founded the World Wide Web Consortium at the Laboratory of Computer Science (LCS) at the Massachusetts Institute of Technology in Boston to regulate its future development and to protect its democratic spirit. He has served as director of the consortium since then. He also works as a senior research scientist at LCS which has now become the Computer Science and Artificial Intelligence Laboratory.

Now based at MIT in Boston as director of the World Wide Web Consortium, Tim Berners-Lee has been able to safeguard the spirit of his original invention and to plan the next phase of the web's development which, he argues, will be even more exciting.

His 1999 book *Weaving the Web* described the Web's birth and growth.

In 2003, Queen Elizabeth II announced that Berners-Lee would be made a Knight Commander of the Order of the British Empire (KBE) for his work on the Web. In 2004, Berners-Lee was awarded the first Millennium Technology Prize, a Finland-based award for excellence which carries a cash prize of one million Euros.

❖❖❖

95

Mother Teresa

(1910-1997)

Mother Teresa was an Albanian Roman Catholic nun with Indian citizenship who founded the Missionaries of Charity in Kolkata, India in 1950. She won the Nobel Peace Prize in 1979 and Bharat Ratna in 1980 for her humanitarian work. She was formally beatified in October 2003 by Pope John Paul II and is now known as Blessed Teresa of Calcutta.

Mother Teresa was born Gonxha (Agnes) Bojaxhiu in Skopje, Yugoslavia, on August 27, 1910.

Much of her young life was centred in the Church. During her early years, however, she was fascinated with stories of missionary life and service.

At 18, she left home for the Loreto Convent in Rathfarnam, Ireland, where she was admitted as a postulant and received the name of Teresa, after her patroness, St. Therese of Lisieux. She was sent by the Loreto order to India and arrived in Calcutta on 6 January 1929. She joined the Loreto novitiate in Darjeeling. She made her final profession as a Loreto nun on 24 May 1937, and hereafter was called Mother Teresa.

She was sent to St. Mary's Bengali Medium School for girls in Calcutta. Here she began a career teaching history and geography for the next 15 years. It was in the protected environment of this school for the daughters of the wealthy that Teresa's new vocation developed and grew.

On 10 September 1946, on a train journey from Calcutta to Darjeeling, Mother Teresa received what she termed the "call within a call," which was to give rise to the Missionaries of Charity family of Sisters, Brothers, Fathers, and Co-Workers. On October 7, 1950, the new congregation of the Missionaries of Charity was officially erected as a religious institute for the Archdiocese of Calcutta.

Teresa first went to Patna for a few months to prepare for her future work by taking a nursing course. In 1948 she received permission from Pius XII to leave her community and live as an independent nun. So back to Calcutta she went and found a small hovel to rent to begin her new undertaking. Wisely, she started by teaching the children of the slums. She strove to make the children of the poor literate, to teach them basic hygiene. As they grew to know her, she gradually began visiting the poor and ill in their families and others, all crowded together in the surrounding squalid shacks, inquiring about their needs. Within a year, young women volunteered their services and later became the core of her Missionaries of Charity. Others offered food, clothing, use of buildings, medical supplies and money. As support and assistance mushroomed, more and more services became possible to huge numbers of suffering people.

Throughout the 1950s and early 1960s, Mother Teresa expanded the work of the Missionaries of Charity both within Calcutta and throughout India. On 1 February 1965, Pope Paul VI granted the Decree of Praise to the Congregation, raising it to pontifical right. Mother Teresa opened houses in Australia, the Middle East, and North America, and the first novitiate outside Calcutta in London. Despite repeated efforts, however, she was never able to open a foundation in China.

In 1962 she was awarded the Padma Shri Award by the Indian government. In 1979 she was awarded the Nobel Peace Prize. She refused the conventional ceremonial banquet given to laureates, and asked that the $6,000 funds be given to the poor in Calcutta. The other awards include: The first Pope John XXIII Peace Prize. (1971), Kennedy Prize (1971), The Nehru Prize for promotion of international peace and understanding (1972), Albert Schweitzer International Prize (1975), Bharat Ratna, Magsaysay Award, States

Presidential Medal of Freedom (1985), Congressional Gold Medal (1994), Honorary citizenship of the United States (November 16, 1996) and the Templeton Award.

Mother Teresa spoke at the fortieth anniversary of the United Nations General Assembly in October 1985. On Christmas Eve of that year, Mother Teresa opened "Gift of Love" in New York, her first house for AIDS patients.

Finally, on September 5, 1997, after finishing her dinner and prayers, she died peacefully. She was formally beatified in October 2003 by Pope John Paul II and is now known as Blessed Teresa of Calcutta.

❖❖❖

96
Margaret Thatcher
(1925-)

Margaret Hilda Thatcher a politician is a former British prime minister as also a former Leader of the Conservative Party from 1975 to 1990. Known as "The Iron Lady" she is the only woman to have held either post.

Margaret Thatcher was born on October 13, 1925 in Grantham, England.

She attended the local grammar school and then Somerville College, Oxford, where she earned a chemistry degree (1947). She developed an early interest in politics, and was president of the student Conservative Association. She worked for four years as a research chemist, but she studied law when not in work and became a barrister in 1954.

Thatcher first stood for Parliament in 1950, but won her first election campaign in 1959, winning the "seat" of Finchley in London, which she held until she retired in 1992. She rose within the ranks of the Conservative Party, and entered the Shadow Cabinet in 1967.

In 1970 she became the Minister for Education, but she rose to public prominence after cancelling a programme providing free milk to primary school children which led to the nickname 'Thatcher the Milk Snatcher'.

She became prime minister in May 1979, when the Conservatives won the majority of seats. In June 1987, her

Conservative Party won its third consecutive general election victory.

Britain's economy in 1979 was in a poor state, and Thatcher's first term in office saw her adopt an economic theory known as Monetarism, while stripping away government regulations on business and subsidies. Many inefficient businesses failed as a result, leading to a rise in unemployment, and inflation doubled. This she countered with a rise in taxes and a change in the money supply, bringing a sharp fall in inflation and opposition from economists and the public.

Argentina invaded the Falklands, a British island in the southern hemisphere. The ensuing Falklands War, which Thatcher ran victoriously, boosted the popularity of her government hugely, leading to the Conservatives winning a large majority at the General Election in 1983.

The Thatcher government set about privatising most of the industries run by the government, including water, electricity and the trains, selling them off relatively cheaply to new private companies. She also clamped down heavily on trade unions, passing laws designed to curb strikes, closed shops and sympathy strikes.

In 1984, Britain's miners protested the government closure of "uneconomic" pits. Thatcher forced them back into work with no concessions. Other aspects of Thatcherism included selling council houses to tenants, reducing social service expenses, limits on print money and a dislike of growing European federalism. She also lowered taxes.

Forging a close relationship with US President Ronald Reagan, Margaret Thatcher expressed strong anti-communism. She was criticised for keeping the Cold War alive by this approach until Gorbachev arrived in Russia to end it. However, she received Gorbachev warmly. Ironically, the Soviet Union gave her the nickname Iron Lady.

In 1984 Margaret Thatcher narrowly survived the IRA bombing of a hotel in Brighton, part of a larger campaign by the IRA for a united and independent Ireland which was, in turn, part of the larger political unrest and violence over British-controlled Northern Ireland.

Her victory in the General Election of 1987 revealed a nation deeply divided, with almost no Tory support in inner cities. Her third term was marked by two chief friction points: a strong opposition to European union, which divided her party, and the "Community Charge", otherwise known as the "Poll Tax", which was so unpopular it caused riots in the streets.

The immediate issue that brought about Thatcher's resignation as prime minister was her unyielding opposition to European integration. She aligned her foreign policy with Washington rather than Europe in the belief that a special relationship existed with the United States. In economic matters, she firmly rejected proposals for a single European currency. Thatcher's "Little England" feelings towards Europe antagonised many voters, including a large number of Conservatives. It was Howe's, the deputy leader of the party, resignation that produced the leadership crisis and Major's emergence as prime minister.

On March 7, 1991 Thatcher received the U.S. Medal of Freedom from President Bush. In 1992 she left her parliamentary seat and became Baroness of Kestevan, taking a place in the House of Lords, as well as speaking publicly round the world. In 1995 she became a member of the Order of the Garter. A series of minor strokes caused her to retire from public speaking in 2002.

❖❖❖

97

Desmond Tutu

(1931-)

Desmond Mpilo Tutuis, a South African cleric and activist, rose to worldwide fame during the 1980s as an opponent of apartheid. In 1984, he became the second South African to be awarded the Nobel Peace Prize. He was elected and ordained the first black South African Anglican Archbishop of Cape Town, South Africa, and primate of the Church of the Province of Southern Africa (now the Anglican Church of Southern Africa).

Desmond Tutu was born on 7 October 1931 in Klerksdorp, South Africa.

Tutu was born a Methodist but became an Anglican when his family changed religions. The Tutu family moved to Johannesburg, South Africa, when Desmond Tutu was twelve years old. He wanted to become a doctor, but because his family could not afford the schooling, he became a teacher.

When the government instituted a system of racially discriminatory education in 1957, a system that would separate black students from white students, Tutu left teaching and entered the Anglican Church. Ordained (declared a priest) in 1961.

He earned a bachelor of arts degree in 1962 from the University of South Africa, and then a master's degree from the University of

London. From 1970 to 1974 he lectured at the University of Lesotho, Botswana, and Swaziland. In 1975 he became dean of Johannesburg, a position from which he publicly challenged white rule.

He became bishop of Lesotho in 1976, and in 1985 bishop of Johannesburg. A short fourteen months later, in April 1986, he was elected archbishop of Cape Town, South Africa, the first black person to head the Anglican Church in southern Africa.

Tutu became one of South Africa's most outspoken critics of apartheid. His international recognition as a critic of apartheid came when he became first General Secretary of the South African Council of Churches in 1978. He spoke out both in South Africa and abroad, often comparing apartheid to Nazism and communism. As a result the government twice revoked his passport, and he was jailed briefly in 1980 after a protest march. Another issue Tutu faced was whether other nations should be urged to apply economic sanctions against South Africa.

In 1984 he was awarded the Nobel Peace Prize, for his "role as a unifying leader figure in the campaign to resolve the problem of apartheid in South Africa".

In 1989 FW De Klerk introduced reforms, which led to the downfall of apartheid and the release of Nelson Mandela. Mandela appointed Tutu to be head of the Truth and Reconciliation committee, which sought to deal with crimes, committed during the apartheid era. This proved to be a difficult process uncovering many painful experiences.

In 1997 Tutu received the Robie Award for his work in humanitarianism. In August 2001, Tutu returned to South Africa after two years in the United States undergoing cancer treatment.

Tutu often speaks out on behalf of oppressed groups around the world. He has been a noted supporter of the Palestinian cause, and the people of East Timor. Recently he criticised the mistreatment of prisoners at Guantanamo Bay and Robert Mugabe's dictatorship in Zimbabwe.

Tutu coined the phrase 'Rainbow Nation' and firmly believes in the possibility of interracial harmony in South Africa.

❖❖❖

98

Swami Vivekananda

(1863-1902)

Swami Vivekananda, born Narendranath Dutta, was the chief disciple of Ramakrishna Paramahamsa and the founder of Ramakrishna Mission. To the World Parliament of Religions he offered a message of a shared spirituality and the harmony of world religions which won the hearts and minds of many seekers; and his vision is still treasured today. He played a major role in spiritual enlightenment of Indian masses and spread Vedanta philosophy in the West.

Swami Vivekananda was born on January 12, 1863 in Calcutta. He was named Narendranath.

As a child Narendra was very lively and naughty. He was good in studies as well as in games. He studied instrumental and vocal music and also practised meditation from a very early age.

In 1879, Narendra passed matriculation and entered Presidency College, Calcutta. After one year, he joined the Scottish Church College, Calcutta and studied philosophy. He studied western logic, Western philosophy and history of European nations.

He joined the Brahmo Samaj, an important religious movement of the time, led by Keshab Chandra Sen, in the pursuit of realising God. During this time he came to know of Sri Ramakrishna Paramahamsa of Dakshineswar. He went to Dakshineswar to see him. He asked Ramakrishna, whether he had seen God. The instantaneous answer from Ramakrishna was, "Yes, I have seen

God, just as I see you here, only in a more clear sense." Narendra was astounded and puzzled. He could feel the man's words were honest and uttered from depths of experience. He started visiting Ramakrishna frequently.

In the beginning the reasoning mind of Vivekananda was sceptical of this God-intoxicated Saint and Vivekananda would frequently question and debate his teachings. However, slowly the spiritual magnetism of Sri Ramakrishna melted his heart and he began to experience the real spirituality that Ramakrishna exuded. Thus Vivekananda's mental opposition faded away to be replaced by an intense surrender to the Divine Mother and a burning longing for realisation. For a short but intense period of about five years, he learnt directly from his Master Sri Ramakrishna, the Advaita Vedanta, the philosophy of non-dualism.

Sri Ramakrishna passed away in 1886 and nominated Narendra as his successor. After his death the other disciples looked to Vivekananda for leadership and he helped form the first monastic order of Ramakrishna. Under his constant guidance he urged his fellow brother disciples to renounce the world and seek communion with God.

In 1890, Narendra set out on a long journey, covering Varanasi, Ayodhya, Agra, Vrindavan, Alwar etc. Narendra acquired the name of Swami Vivekananda during the journey, given by Maharaja of Khetri for his discrimination of things, good and bad. He came in close contact with the cultures of different regions of India and various classes of people in India. He observed the imbalance in society and tyranny in the name of caste. He realised the need for a national rejuvenation if India was to survive at all.

In 1893, Swami Vivekananda represented Hinduism at the first World Parliament of Religions in Chicago. At the opening ceremony Vivekananda was one of the last speakers to speak The previous speakers had talked about the merits of their own religion but Vivekananda appealed to the whole audience with his vision of oneness and equality before God He earned wild applause for beginning his address with the famous words, "Sisters and brothers of America." He mesmerised everyone in America with his masterful oratory. However he did not try in any way to prove the superiority of his religion. Instead he spoke with great sincerity about the harmony of world religions and the common spirituality of humanity. It was this universal message of oneness which captivated the audience. Wherever he went, he dwelt at length on the greatness of Indian culture. He spoke with spontaneous ease on every topic, be it History, Sociology, Philosophy or Literature. He talked about the ancient tradition of Vedanta and his hope of fusing the spirituality of the East with the materialism of the West.

Swami Vivekananda also went to England. Many people became his disciples. One notable example was Miss Margaret Noble (later named Nivedita), originally from Ireland. Nivedita was to become a devoted disciple who would dedicate her life to the Indian people.

Swami Vivekananda returned to India in 1897 and started disseminating the message of spiritual development among Indians. He realised that social service was possible only through the concerted efforts on an organised mission, and so started Sri Ramakrishna Mission in 1897, formulating its ideology and goal.

During the next two years he bought a site at Belur on the banks of the Ganga, constructed the buildings and established the Ramakrishna Mutt. He once again toured the West from January 1899 to December 1900. He founded the Ramakrishna Order in 1898.

His lectures, writings, letters, and poems are published as *The Complete Works of Swami Vivekananda.*

Swami Vivekananda died at the young age of 39 on July 4, 1902 at Belur Mutt near Calcutta.

❖❖❖

99

Oprah Winfrey

(1954-)

Oprah Gail Winfrey is an American television presenter, media mogul and philanthropist. Her internationally-syndicated talk show, The Oprah Winfrey Show, has earned her multiple Emmy Awards. She is also an influential book critic, an Academy Award nominated actress, and a magazine publisher.

Oprah Gail Winfrey was born on January 29, 1954 in Kosciusko, Mississippi.

For the first six years of her life, the young Winfrey was raised on a Mississippi farm by her grandmother. Here she was taught to read at a very early age, instilling a love of reading in her that she retains today. She began her public speaking career at the tender age of three when she began reading aloud and reciting sermons to the congregation of her church.

From age six to 13, she lived in Milwaukee with her mother. After suffering abuse and molestation, she ran away and was sent to a juvenile detention home at the age of 13, only to be denied admission because all the beds were filled. As a last resort, she was sent to Nashville to live under her father's strict discipline. Before she ceased her promiscuous and wild behaviour, she became pregnant and gave birth to a stillborn baby boy when she was fourteen. The death of her baby devastated her and she vowed to turn her life around. Her father helped her with her mission by strapping her with his strict rules and discipline. He made sure that she stuck to her curfew, maintained high grades in school and encouraged her to be her best.

Oprah's broadcasting career began at 17, when she was hired by WVOL radio in Nashville, and two years later signed on with WTVF-TV in Nashville, the first black African American woman television news anchor to work in Nashville on the WTVF-TV station at a tender age.

Shortly afterwards, she entered Tennessee State University where she majored in Speech Communications and Performing Arts. She won several pageants, including "Miss Black Nashville" and "Miss Tennessee".

In 1976, she moved to Baltimore to join WJZ-TV news as a co-anchor, and in 1978 discovered her talent for hosting talk shows when she became co-host of WJZ-TV's "People Are Talking", while continuing to serve as anchor and news reporter. The show was a hit and Winfrey stayed for eight years.

In January 1984, she came to Chicago to host WLS-TV's "AM Chicago", a faltering local talk show, competing against the immensely popular Phil Donahue Show. After several months, Oprah's warm-hearted style turned "AM Chicago" into the hottest show in town. The format was soon expanded to one hour, and in September 1985 it was renamed "The Oprah Winfrey Show". Seen nationally since September 8, 1986, "The Oprah Winfrey Show" became the number one talk show in national syndication in less than a year. Her success led to a role in Steven Spielberg's 1985 adaptation of Alice Walker's novel, *The Color Purple* in 1985. Her performance earned her nominations for an Oscar and Golden Globe Award in the category of Best Supporting Actress. Critics again lauded her performance in *Native Son*, a movie adaptation of Richard Wright's classic 1940 novel.

In June 1987, in its first year of eligibility, "The Oprah Winfrey Show" received three Daytime Emmy Awards in the categories of Outstanding Host, Outstanding Talk/Service Programme and Outstanding Direction. In June 1988, "The Oprah Winfrey Show" received its second consecutive Daytime Emmy Award as Outstanding Talk/Service Programme, and she herself received the International Radio and Television Society's "Broadcaster of the Year" Award. She was the youngest person and only the fifth woman ever to receive the honor in IRTS's 25-year history.

Her love of acting and her desire to bring quality entertainment projects into production prompted her to form her own production company, HARPO Productions, Inc., in 1986. The following year, HARPO produced it first television mini series, *The Women of Brewster Place,* with Oprah Winfrey as star and Executive Producer. It has been followed by the TV movies *There Are No Children Here* (1993), and *Before Women Had Wings* (1997), which she both produced and appeared in. In 1998, she starred in the feature film *Beloved,* from the book by the Nobel Prize-winning American author Toni Morrison.

In 1991, motivated in part by her memories of childhood abuse, she initiated a campaign to establish a national database of convicted child abusers, and testified before a U.S. Senate Judiciary Committee on behalf of a National Child Protection Act. President Clinton signed the "Oprah Bill" into law in 1993, establishing the national database she had sought, which is now available to law enforcement agencies and concerned parties across the country.

Oprah Winfrey was named one of the 100 Most Influential People of the 20th Century by *Time* magazine, and in 1998 received a Lifetime Achievement Award from the National Academy of Television Arts and Sciences. Her influence extended to the publishing industry when she began her on-air book club. Oprah Book Club selections became instant bestsellers, and in 1999 she received the National Book Foundation's 50th anniversary gold medal for her service to books and authors.

She is one of the partners in Oxygen Media, Inc., a cable channel and interactive network presenting programming designed primarily for women. She is the founder of the successful *O,* the Oprah Magazine.

In 2000, Oprah's Angel Network began presenting a $100,000 "Use Your Life Award" to people who are using their lives to improve the lives of others. When *Forbes* magazine published its list of America's billionaires for the year 2003, it disclosed that Oprah Winfrey was the first African-American woman to become a billionaire.

❖❖❖

100

Tiger Woods

(1975-)

Eldrick Tont "Tiger" Woods is an American professional golfer who ranks among the most successful golfers of all time. He is the youngest man ever, and the first man of colour, to win the Masters Tournament of golf.

Tiger Woods was born Eldrick Woods on December 30, 1975, in Cypress, California. Earl Woods gave his son Eldrick the nickname 'Tiger', after a soldier and friend of his who was also nicknamed Tiger in his days as a lieutenant colonel in the U.S. Army.

Tiger grew up in Cypress, California, where he would watch his father hit golf balls and would mimic his father's swing while still young.

At the mere age of two, Tiger played with comedian and golfer Bob Hope. He was featured in *Golf Digest* and on the popular television show *That's Incredible!* at age five, after having already succeeded in shooting 48 for nine holes while the same children his age were still playing with building blocks.

A six-time winner at the Optimist International Junior Tournament, Tiger won at the ages of eight and nine, and consecutively from ages 12 to 15. Media accounts of the boy prodigy had reached nearly legendary proportions by 1994, when he entered Stanford University as a freshman on a full golf scholarship.

While a student at Stanford University, he won 10 collegiate events and held the NCAA title.

When he was 17 years old, Tiger played in a professional tournament the Nissan Los Angeles Open in 1992. One year later, he participated in three PGA Tour events and in 1994, Tiger was placed 34th in the 1994 Johnnie Walker Asian Classic in Thailand and appeared in three more PGA Tours that same year.

After having won the 1994 Western Amateur and representing the United States in the 1994 World Amateur Team Championships in France, during his first year of college, he won the U.S. Amateur title and qualified to play in the Masters tournament in Augusta, Georgia, in the spring of 1995. He won the 1995 Walker Cup Match in Wales. He was ready for his first major championships in 1995 — the Masters and The British Open.

By 1996, Woods had won three U.S. Amateur titles, one after another, an amazing accomplishment in itself. In August of 1996, he quit college in order to play professional golf. *Sports Illustrated* named him 1996 "Sportsman of the Year," and by January of 1997, he had already won three professional tournaments. He was a media sensation.

In April of 1997, only eight months into his professional career, he played in the prestigious (important and famous) Masters tournament held at Georgia's Augusta National Golf Club. When the tournament was over, Woods had made history as the youngest person ever to win the Masters title. His score was an unprecedented 270 strokes. His victory margin set another record—twelve strokes ahead of the runner-up. This feat was enhanced by the fact that Woods was the first man of colour ever to win the title.

In 1997, Tiger had won the first Mercedes Champion-ships of the season, the Masters and four PGA events. Tiger became the leading money winner, winning $2, 440, 831. Less than three months passed until July 6, 1997, when he won the Western Open, another major golf tournament.

In 1999 Woods achieved the greatest moment in his career

when he won the PGA Championship by one shot. He continued his success in November 1999 when he shot the best total ever in the World Cup, helping to lead the United States to victory in the tournament. He was also named the PGA Tour Player of the Year for the second time on November 30, 1999.

On January 9, 2000, Woods won the Mercedes Championship. It was his fifth consecutive victory and, at the time, golf's longest winning streak in forty-six years. On February 7, 2000, he extended that streak by winning the Pebble Beach National Pro-Am. He became the first player since Ben Hogan (1912–1997) in 1948 to win six straight tour events. He went on to win the Bay Hill Invitational on March 19, 2000. On June 18, 2000, he won the U.S. Open, his third major championship. The next month, on July 23, he won the British Open, thus winning the Grand Slam. He became the youngest player to win all four major championships and just the fifth ever.

On April 8, 2001, Woods won the sixty-fifth Masters Tournament at the Augusta National Golf Club. The win made him the only golfer in history to hold the four major championship titles at the same time.

Woods won the sixty-sixth Masters Tournament on April 14, 2002. At the turn of the twenty-first century, Woods was the most dominant figure in all of sports, and his name will surely be decorated throughout the record books before his career is over. Cementing his reputation as Nicklaus's heir, Woods won the British Open in 2005, the year of Nicklaus's final appearance at the competition. Although 2005 and 2006 were tough on Woods — his father died 3 May 2006 — he won the British Open again in 2006, and the PGA Championship in both 2006 and 2007.

Woods has won all the major tournaments at least twice: The Masters in 1997, 2001, 2002 and 2005, the PGA Championship in 1999, 2000, 2006 and 2007, the British Open in 2000, 2005 and 2006, and the U.S. Open in 2000, 2002 and 2008.

In February 2008, Tiger Woods won his third WGC Match Play Championship title with a record 8 & 7 win over Stewart Cink. It was Tiger's sixth straight tournament success. He then followed up by winning the Arnold Palmer Invitational. In June 2008, Tiger Woods, playing with an injured knee, won the US Open. It was his 14th major title.

❖❖❖

Other Books on
GENERAL SERIES

1. Art of Joyful Living **(New)**
2. Chanakya Neeti **(New)**
3. Helpline for Stressed Parents **(New)**
4. Grow Rich with Peace of Mind **(New)**
5. How to be Fit and Young **(New)**
6. How to Succeed in Life **(New)**
7. 100 Ways to Develop Self Confidence
8. Child Development
9. Abraham Lincoln A Complete Biography
10. Mein Kampf My Struggle
11. Think and Grow Rich
12. The Art of Personality Development
13. Positive Mind Power
14. Travel & Tourism An Industry Facilitator
15. World's Great Authors And Poets
16. Effective Editing Help Yourself in Becoming a Good Editor
17. Smart House-Keeping for Modern Women
18. Develop Super Power Memory
19. World's Great Personalities
20. Personality Plus
21. Power of Positive Thinking
22. Art of Successful Parenting
23. A Handbook of Etiquettes
24. World's Great Scientists
25. Body Language
26. Art of Successful Living
27. Jokes for All

28. Selected Dohas
29. Baby Names for Girls **(New)**
30. Baby Names for Boys **(New)**
31. Art of Public Speaking
32. The World's Greatest Speeches
33. Group Discussions
34. Personality Development
35. Think Positive & Things Will Go Right
36. Once in a Blue Moon (A Tantra Tale)
37. God is Dead
38. Travel India (A Complete Guide for Tourists)
39. Glimpses of Urdu Poetry
40. How to Reduce Tension
41. A Book of Stenography
42. Baby Names for the Boy
43. Baby Names for the Girl
44. Ripples in Tranquil Waters

Lotus PRESS

Unit No. 220, 2nd Floor, 4735/22, Prakash Deep Building,
Ansari Road, Darya Ganj, New Delhi- 110002

• E-mail : lotuspress1984@gmail.com, www.lotuspress.co.in